GIOVANNI BELLINI'S ST. FRANCIS

IN THE FRICK COLLECTION

GIOVANNI BELLINI'S

ST. FRANCIS

IN THE FRICK COLLECTION

BY MILLARD MEISS

Published for The Frick Collection, New York, by

PRINCETON UNIVERSITY PRESS · 1964

CONTENTS

LIST OF PLATES

23 Titian, *Pesaro Altarpiece*. Venice, Frari.

24 Mantegna, *Agony in the Garden*. Tours, Musée des Beaux-Arts.

25 Fra Filippo Lippi, *Madonna*. Florence, Uffizi.

26 Giovanni Bellini, *Descent into Limbo*. Bristol, City Art Gallery.

27 Giambono, *Stigmatization of St. Francis* (detail). Venice, Count Vittorio Cini.

28 Giovanni Battista Tiepolo, *Stigmatization of St. Francis* (detail). London, Count A. Seilern.

29 Piero della Francesca, *Members of a Confraternity* (detail of *Madonna*). Borgo Sansepolcro, Museo.

30 Antonello da Messina, *Crucifixion* (detail). London, National Gallery.

31 Giovanni Bellini, *Coronation of the Virgin*. Pesaro, Museo Civico.

32 Giovanni Bellini, *Coronation of the Virgin* (detail). Pesaro, Museo Civico.

33 Giovanni Bellini (assisted), *Resurrection*. Berlin-Dahlem, Museum Dahlem.

34 Giovanni Bellini (assisted), *St. Jerome*. Florence, Contini Collection.

35 Carlo Crivelli, *St. Jerome*. London, National Gallery.

36 Giovanni Bellini, *St. Jerome* (predella of Figure 31). Pesaro, Museo Civico.

37 Giovanni Bellini, *St. Jerome*. Birmingham, Barber Institute.

38 Garofalo, *The Baptist*. Cambridge, Fitzwilliam Museum.

39 Bartolommeo della Gatta, *Stigmatization of St. Francis*. Castiglion Fiorentino, Pinacoteca.

40 Giovanni Bellini, *Stigmatization of St. Francis* (predella of Figure 31). Pesaro, Museo Civico.

41 Site of the Stigmatization, La Verna.

42 Marco Zoppo, *Stigmatization of St. Francis*. Baltimore, Walters Gallery.

43 Domenico Ghirlandaio, *Stigmatization of St. Francis*. Florence, S. Trinita.

44 Giovanni Bellini, *Agony in the Garden*. London, National Gallery.

45 Follower of Guido da Siena, *Stigmatization of St. Francis*. Siena, Pinacoteca.

46 Florentine, late fifteenth century, *Stigmatization of St. Francis*. Modena, Galleria Estense.

47 Barocci (assisted), *Stigmatization of St. Francis*. Florence, Uffizi.

48 Ercole de' Roberti, *Agony in the Garden*. Dresden, Gemäldegalerie.

49 Giovanni Bellini, *Agony in the Garden* (detail of Figure 44). London, National Gallery.

50 Dirk Bouts, *God the Father* (detail of *Gathering of Manna*). Louvain, St. Peter's.

[8]

FOREWORD

I FIRST SAW the painting that is the subject of this essay in 1928. I have been looking at it from time to time ever since, and occasionally it still presents novel aspects. The richness of the work, rare though it is, was not, however, the only source of its attraction. My curiosity was stirred by the enigma of the content, especially when it became evident that the painting is one of several in which a great master wrought related changes in traditional themes. The picture offers thus an opportunity to observe the interplay of some of the larger concerns that guided Bellini's work during those two decades of his career that proved so momentous for Venetian and indeed all European painting.

Mr. Franklin Biebel, director of the Frick Collection, has for several years shared my interest in the problems presented by Bellini's painting, and I am deeply indebted to him for facilitating my study in every possible way. I have profited from discussions of the painting with him and with two other friends, Craig H. Smyth and Howard McP. Davis. Mr. William Suhr, conservator of the Frick Collection, generously made many helpful comments on technique and problems of condition. I am grateful to Messrs. James Bush-Brown, Edward J. Alexander, associate curator of the New York Botanical Garden, and Dr. John Fogg, Department of Botany, University of Pennsylvania, for identifying numerous plants in Bellini's picture. They recognized many of them immediately, so accurate is the painter's portrayal. For the identification of the birds Mr. John H. Baker kindly set me on the right track. They are wonderfully observed, especially the pose of the bittern, though Bellini of course did not seek the precision of Audubon.

M. M.

May, 1963

[11]

Giovanni Bellini, St. Francis. Detail, The Saint and his garden.

GIOVANNI BELLINI'S ST. FRANCIS

Y EARS AGO, when an exclusively secular view of Renaissance culture was much more widely held than it is today, the masterpieces of Renaissance art were valued for their qualities of form and for their contributions to the "discovery of man and nature," as Jakob Burckhardt put it.[1] Thus in Giovanni Bellini's panel in the Frick Collection, one of the most beautiful paintings of the Quattrocento, it was the landscape, and often nothing but the landscape, that stirred the enthusiasm of critics (Fig. 1). Mr. Berenson, for instance, who gave us the first and still the fullest account of the picture, wrote in 1916 that the painter himself as well as his client must have understood the picture as pure landscape. For both, he said, St. Francis was nothing more than a necessary pious pretext.[2]

While everyone today shares Mr. Berenson's enthusiasm for Bellini's painting of nature, few I think would accept his estimate of the picture as a whole or of the role of the saint in it. It does not seem so easy now to avert one's glance from this ecstatic figure, his arms spread wide, his head and body bent backwards, his mouth open as he looks up to heaven — awed, anguished, and with the unfathomable darkness of passion that had already clouded the faces of similar saints by Masaccio and Donatello. Titian himself was deeply impressed by this figure; his St. Francis in the Pesaro Altarpiece assures us of that (Fig. 23). In this later version the saint is far less tense, but he has retained the physiognomy, the gesture, the movement of the fingers of the right hand, and even much of the pattern of folds in the habit. Amidst the massive figures of Titian's developed style the St. Francis has a strikingly Quattrocento, early Bellinesque look. The position of the two hands continued to be associated with St. Francis, and particularly with the Stigmatization, as late as the eighteenth century, in for example the painting of Tiepolo (Fig. 28).[3] It is imitable elements like this, as well as a way of seeing, that constitute the Venetian — or indeed any other — tradition.

Altogether, we feel, Bellini's saint is one of the most moving portrayals of religious rapture in Christian art. But what is the significance of the saint's transport? Is it ideal and timeless, or is there some specific occasion for it? Scholars have bestowed on the painting a variety of titles. They have called it The Ecstasy of St. Francis,[4] or St. Francis in the Desert,[5] The Stigmatization of St. Francis[6] or a moment just after it,[7] or simply St. Francis.[8] All of this reflects uncertainty. What is surprising, however, is not the lack of conviction — indeed the present essay will not offer definitive proof — but the absence of any discussion of the question itself. In fact, given the rare beauty and great historical importance of the painting, the literature on *any* aspect of it is remarkably scanty.

In the developing art of landscape painting Bellini's *St. Francis* had already been preceded in the fifteenth century by several extraordinary portrayals of nature, notably Domenico Veneziano's *tondo* in Berlin, the *Baptism* by Piero della Francesca in London, and Fra Angelico's *Visitation* in Cortona, which is based on a specific view of the Umbrian plain. Bellini's picture is thus certainly not the first great Italian accomplishment in this field, but it is undoubtedly the richest. Only outside the peninsula, in Netherlandish paintings, does landscape exhibit a similar wealth of natural forms. Now Bellini undoubtedly knew works by Jan van Eyck, Roger, or their circle,[9] and these paintings offered him not only descriptions of a marvellously luminous, multiform world but a novel technique with which to portray it. This technique is based on the addition of a slow-drying substance, probably oil, to the fast-drying tempera. Bellini began to alter his medium in the early 'seventies, for the first time on a large scale in the Pesaro *Coronation* (Fig. 31).[10] The Frick panel, which is generally placed between 1479 and 1485 but which may well, I believe, have been painted a few years earlier, shows a greater mastery of it. The colors are more extensively fused, but Bellini still tends to hold them rather separate and to lay them in patches or bands, in the manner of a tempera painter. This tempera-like practice is especially conspicuous in the delineation of the flanks of the distant hills.

It is not simply a new vehicle that produces the soft glow of Bellini's painting. In most areas of the picture, and particularly in all the masses of rock, he has laid the shades and shadows as well as the green vegetation over a layer of light blue-green. Earlier, shaded surfaces and deep hues were not prepared in a light but a dark color, and though Masaccio and his followers began to disregard this time-honored convention it was Bellini, following Flemish precedent, who decisively reversed it. The darker areas within the rocks acquire thereby a depth and luminosity unprecedented in Italian painting. These qualities are enhanced by Bellini's method, inspired too by the Netherlanders, of glazing, of painting for instance a layer of green and then laying over it a transparent brown. Inasmuch as the glaze could be spread or wiped unevenly, as in the crown of the large tree, the painter could vary the quality of a green by altering either the pigment or the film over it. With these techniques Bellini achieved a novel glowing depth of color. The atmosphere acquired a greater vibrancy, and the diffusion of light could become a major pictorial theme. Altogether the work heralds a new era in the history of painting.

The encyclopaedic variety of nature in the Frick panel is controlled by a broad, salient geometric structure, clear evidence of a Tuscan and Central Italian inheritance. Bellini's art at this moment combines, then, essential qualities of the two great traditions of fifteenth-century Europe, the Flemish and the Tuscan. It becomes a sort of *summa* of Quattrocento pictorial experience. This is for Bellini a time of intensive study and continuous change, but there is of course already much in his art that is wholly fresh and personal. In the work of none of his predecessors, particularly his Italian predecessors, is there a comparable union of figure and landscape. This aspect of Bellini's painting is readily disclosed by comparison with the composition that most closely approaches it, and which may have served as a model — Mantegna's *Agony in the Garden* in Tours, painted between 1456 and 1459 for the predella of the S. Zeno, Verona, altarpiece (Fig. 24).

[14]

The theme of Mantegna's panel is similar, involving a figure in a landscape engaged in supernatural colloquy, and the design is closely related. The figure appears at the right, gazing tensely upward with open mouth. Beyond is a great mass of rock, while the ground immediately behind him declines in a long slope towards the left frame of the picture. Above this declining plane rises a hill. It is crossed by roads, it has a town on its flank, and it is crowned by a castle. In the left foreground of the two compositions stands a large tree,[11] and nearby in both water gushes from a carved stone spout.

Despite the sheer rockiness of Mantegna's landscape in the region occupied by the figures, nature is not entirely hostile to them. It offers many small fruits. It casts up for Christ a sort of primitive altar. It provides for one apostle who sleeps a conveniently inclined, though uncomfortably hard, natural cot, and it gives indomitable St. Peter a stony pillow. Thus Mantegna's world, though severe, makes concessions to its inhabitants, assuming here and there, by a strange ambiguous process, the shape of constructed objects. For this reason no doubt its inhabitants do not find it wholly uncongenial. They also seem to feel the familiarity with stone, or indeed the affection for it, that is so important a part of the Italian cultural heritage.

At the outset of his career Giovanni Bellini's conception of nature was much influenced by Mantegna's, but for him the world was always gentler and more responsive to the people in it. Around the time of painting the Frick panel he had largely resolved Mantegna's ambiguity of the natural and the artificial, replacing it by a close, fruitful association of the two. St. Francis stands in a sort of elementary amphitheatre, partly natural and partly man-made. Behind him there is a low, curving wall. Whether the stones in it were once cut by hand or simply found in the rocky environs, they were certainly laid up manually in this wall. The builder, perhaps the saint himself, has filled with earth the pocket between the wall and the crag (Fig. 11). Mullein, juniper, and orris root grow luxuriantly in this earth, kept moist, it would seem, by water carried from the spring in the saint's jug. At the left the wall merges with a fault in the rock that tends to prolong its curve to the edge of the cliff.

This joining of the natural and the artificial is apparent also in the sort of little hedgerow that discreetly screens the saint and his habitation from the world beyond. For most of its length it consists of brambles that seem to flourish naturally in this arid place. But at the extreme left it is terminated by a regular row of shoots that, though apparently springing from the roots of the laurel tree, seem expressly pruned, if not indeed planted, to complete the fence (Fig. 5). Similarly the slender willow branches, all of one size, that have been cut and woven to form a gate to the saint's cell have burst into life again and sprout leaves (Fig. 15).

Just behind the saint the massive vertical rock seems to melt in accommodation, forming a natural spreading niche that repeats the shape of his figure. In front of him the rocks take on a sort of tidal character, ebbing and flowing as though they were impelled by the depth of his experience. These swirling rocks, along with the laurel tree at the left, which is in the line of the saint's gaze, are conspicuous as agitated objects in an otherwise marvellously still world. While these objects in front respond to the excitement of the saint, it is his strength and majesty that are expressed by the crag behind. This crag is divided into three vertical masses, and the profile of the central one repeats the curving profile of the saint. This central mass, moreover, is not blue-green like the others; a pinkish light falls on it, very much as on the buff habit of the saint. In the distance, in the town, the figure of St. Francis is echoed by the free-standing, sunlit towers.

The landscape is composed of three quite distinct parts: a rocky, cool blue-green foreground, a green grassy middle ground, and a warm yellow-brown distance, overhung by an intense — now almost too intense — blue sky. The composition is similar, as we have said, to Mantegna's *Agony* in Tours, but in one respect it is utterly different. Both the near and distant hills slope in the same direction, so that the design is decisively asymmetrical.[12] This movement of masses is countered by the essentially coloristic diagonal of the saint, the lectern, and the similarly warm hills in the distance. Still, the asymmetry and the compositional movement are such that without the figure of the saint, relatively small though it is, the design is unsatisfactory. The figure is vital to the balance and coherence of the composition as a whole, and it is effective not so much as shape or color but as actor. Most important of all is the glance, directed towards the upper left corner of the picture with such intensity that it balances all the opposing diagonals of the design. It is strengthened by the orthogonals of the trellis and the lectern and, still more, by the location of the vanishing point in the upper left margin of the painting, near the prominent curve in the trunk of the tree.

Bellini's asymmetrical composition, moving from lower left to a large mass higher on the right, inaugurates in Venice a tradition that leads to Titian's Frari *Madonna* (Fig. 23). It probably has its roots in the most conspicuous earlier example of a design of this sort, Piero della Francesca's fresco in the Tempio Malatestiano, and it reminds us that only a short time before the painting of this picture Bellini had made a trip to Pesaro that almost certainly took him through Rimini. Around 1473–1475, according to most historians, but perhaps as early as 1470, as we shall see,[13] Bellini was working on the *Coronation of the Virgin* for S. Francesco, Pesaro (Fig. 31), and even if — as seems unlikely — he painted this huge altarpiece in Venice, he must have visited Pesaro before the work was finished. The castle so insistently exhibited in the opening in the throne of the *Coronation* is probably the Rocca di Gradara near Pesaro (Fig. 32).[14] Several specific sites or buildings visible along the way from Venice are represented in paintings made during the next five to ten years. The Ponte d'Augusto in Rimini appears in the *St. Jerome* in the Contini Collection (Fig. 34), and the monuments of nearby Ravenna are visible in the landscapes of the *St. Jerome* and the Naples *Transfiguration* (Fig. 62). The church of S. Vitale may be seen in the Contini panel, and the mausoleum of Theodoric at Ravenna and the campanile of S. Apollinare in Classe in the *Transfiguration*.[15] This kind of travel record is novel in painting.

We do not know whether at this time the painter visited also towns on the other side of the mountains such as Borgo Sansepolcro, Arezzo, and Florence, but the Frick picture shows relationships with paintings in those places. The beautiful gesture of St. Francis, first of all, is essentially novel in Venice,[16] though it was preceded by a lowering of the open hands in Giambono's *Stigmatization* in the Cini Collection (Fig. 27). The pantomime of Bellini's figure is familiar, however, in the work of Piero della Francesca. One of the members of the Confraternity of Mercy kneeling before the Madonna in the Borgo Sansepolcro altarpiece extends his arms similarly (Fig. 29), and so does the youth who is revived when the true cross is held over him in the fresco in S. Francesco,

[16]

Arezzo. Both these figures, though they lack the intensity of Bellini's saint, look upward with a similar religious veneration.[17] The articulation of the hands implies a study of ancient statuary.

In addition to Bellini two other admirers of the art of Piero adopted this broad expressive gesture. Bartolommeo della Gatta employed it for St. Francis in his freshly conceived and, as always, touching panel of the Stigmatization at Castiglion Fiorentino, for which he received a final payment in 1487 (Fig. 80). The hands are so similar to Bellini's, even in detail, that we begin to speculate whether Bartolommeo, whatever he owed Piero, could have known the Frick panel. Such speculation is not checked when we notice the folded cuff of Bartolommeo's saint, so characteristic of Bellini's tunics; nor when we observe in the environment the rounded mound on which the saint stands, the rocks and a cave, the live shoot growing from the cut tree-stump behind the saint, and the two animals (deer?) on the grassy plateau beyond.

Another master, Antonello da Messina, who was studying the work of Piero della Francesca around the same time as Bellini — the two might even have met before one of his pictures — adopted the gesture for a St. John seated below the Cross in a panel painted in 1475, perhaps in Venice (Fig. 30). Antonello and Giambellino gave much to each other, and we cannot exclude the possibility that it was in this process of exchange that the gesture passed from one to the other. In any event, Bellini looked intently at this very *Crucifixion* by Antonello, for its broad planes, its quiet symmetry, and its classical balance are recaptured in his picture of the same subject now in the Corsini Collection in Florence.[18] And Antonello's jewel-like skulls and bones strewn on the arid ground reappear in the later *Crucifixion* from Bellini's workshop in the Niccolini Collection in Florence (Fig. 60).

The Pesaro altarpiece is the first large painting, among surviving works, that presents Bellini's rapidly changing art in a new phase (Fig. 31). In it he carried more deeply his analysis of color and light, guided by Flemish models and, if the altarpiece is after 1475 (as only a few historians nowadays maintain), by Antonello da Messina also.[19] Bellini fused this more evolved "visual intimacy" with a new planar and spatial geometry of color as well as form;[20] this he derived from Piero della Francesca, who at that very time was himself seized with a renewed enthusiasm for the accomplishments of the Netherlanders.[21] It was however not the art of Piero alone to which Bellini responded in his new, more southerly environment. When designing the *Coronation* he rejected decisively the pageantry that had distinguished Venetian representations of the event from the time of Guariento's fresco for the Ducal Palace.[22] Instead of the splendid *cours célestes* of Jacobello or Antonio Vivarini or Giambono[23] Bellini created a simple and sober composition that recalls the Tuscan tradition from the early Trecento through, say, Giovanni di Paolo's panel in the Lehman Collection.[24] Though no Tuscan examples limit the witnesses to as few as four, they characteristically show the throne set directly upon the floor, whereas in Venice it is set high amidst the throng of witnesses.[25] In the Venetian scenes furthermore God the Father usually presides, enthroned between and above Christ and the Virgin. And even in some smaller Venetian pictures of the subject where these features are lacking, Christ and the Virgin are seated before a rich cloth of honor rather than before the back of a throne.[26]

Hints of a study of Tuscan style are offered also by the predella panels: by the *Nativity*, first of all, which shows a plateau-valley type of composition that, though used by Piero for other subjects, including the *St. Jerome* that may even have been visible then in Venice, appears in Nativities by Baldovinetti and other Florentine masters.[27] The *Conversion of St. Paul*, an active, even violent, design very exceptional in the work of Bellini, may imply a cursory study of Florentine experiments with rearing horses that extend from Uccello to Antonio Pollaiuolo.[28] And does not that strange device of opening the throne upon a landscape remind us of Fra Filippo's Uffizi *Madonna* (Fig. 25)? This *Madonna* resembles a relief sculpture, and, as in the *Coronation*, we have the impression that the marble background has been removed to open a window onto nature. Earlier, Jan van Eyck in his *Rolin Madonna* and then Roger van der Weyden in his *St. Luke* had introduced a landscape at the center of a composition, surrounding it however with architecture rather than with furniture or an actual frame.

While these earlier paintings provide precedents for one or another aspect of Bellini's framed view, they do not quite prepare us for its particular form. The landscape is marvellously painted but, rising just above the principal heads, it is greatly distracting (Fig. 32). For once the artist would seem to have lost his good judgment — but only, perhaps, under very strong pressure. If, as seems probable, the castle is the Rocca di Gradara and the painting was commissioned by Alessandro Sforza, lord of Pesaro,[29] Bellini was probably asked to celebrate his capture of the castle from Sigismondo Malatesta in 1463. The building is presented, in any event, as a sort of trophy at the center of the design.

The Pesaro altarpiece, and therefore also Bellini's journey south, are generally dated in the early 'seventies, most often 1473–1475. The painting in the Frick Collection has always been placed later than that and there is, in fact, common agreement that it was made between 1479 and 1485, after the *Resurrection* in Berlin (probably finished ca. 1479 — Fig. 33)[30] and even after — or some believe, just before — the *Transfiguration* in Naples (Fig. 62).[31] This placement of the *St. Francis*, suggested by its chromatic brilliance, raises serious problems. Though some reminiscences of Mantegna are visible in all these works,[32] the *St. Francis* is the most deeply Mantegnesque. Its stratified rocks, vines and other plants may be seen again, though in a less luscious form, in the *Descent into Limbo* in Bristol, which is actually a copy after Mantegna (Fig. 26).[33] Line is more telling in the *St. Francis* than in the other large panels. It defines the tenseness of the saint and of the slender, throbbing trees that rise at both sides of the design. The edges of forms are salient in the rocks of the foreground and in the distant landscape as well. Alongside these hills the hills of the *Resurrection* look soft, fluffy, picturesque — islands of color that glow in the light rather than some denser substance carved, it would seem, into lively relief (Fig. 33). True, the execution of the *Resurrection*, in which the participation of assistants is especially evident, may have extended over several years, so that it was in part contemporary with the *St. Francis*. In any event some forms are similar to the Frick panel or even "older" looking — the tree at the left, the large shield, and perhaps also the astonishing floating cloth of Christ, no doubt a consequence of Bellini's admiration of a picture by Roger van der Weyden, seen probably when passing through Ferrara.[34] The figures in the *Resurrection*, on the other hand, are much broader than the St. Francis and emanate from a more pictorial vision.

[18]

This newer vision is further developed in the *Transfiguration* (Fig. 62). Here the distinction between foreground, middle ground and distance, so decisively preserved in the Frick panel and, to a lesser extent, in the *Resurrection*, has given way to a more direct extension inward through a complex series of intersecting planes. The objects, as well as the patches of light and shade, are scattered more freely through the space, greatly enhancing the picturesqueness of the whole. Alongside this painting and the *Resurrection*, indeed alongside any other work of Bellini, the Frick panel is distinguished by its prominent geometric structure. In no other work are the shapes so firmly organized by repeated diagonals, horizontals, and verticals. The pattern of color is similarly conceived, progressing regularly from cool in the foreground to very warm in the distance — from blue, in other words, through green, to yellow- and red-brown. Then the near blue, which is continued upward in the rocks, is repeated, but with greater intensity, in the sky, completing on three sides a frame of blue for the more varied colors within. While the linearity of this composition reflects the conventions of Mantegna, its bold, firm geometricity would seem to be another consequence of that study of Piero and of Florentine painting which, as we have mentioned, Bellini undertook during his trip southward.[35]

Both the *Resurrection* and the *Transfiguration* seem to imply a wish to loosen and break open the firm, restricting organization of the Pesaro altarpiece and the *St. Francis*. The landscape of the *Resurrection* discloses a delight in the accidental and the surprising, in other words the picturesque, which Bellini admired in Flemish painting. The later *Transfiguration*, devoted more to a flow of color, tends to present broad *taches*, at the sacrifice of an equilibrium between spatial and planar design. It is true that the *Resurrection* still shows, as the *St. Francis* does not, the large brown areas of the Pesaro altarpiece. The distant hills of the *St. Francis* are brighter and warmer, but this, we shall see, is in part at least to be ascribed to the iconography rather than simply to a formal intention. Still, there remains a chromatic richness in the Frick panel that is exceptional in the 'seventies. Perhaps we may conclude that in the great works of this period Bellini was probing different possibilities, and that the *St. Francis*, while early in many respects, predicts the color of the mid 'eighties. The alternative hypothesis, less probable I think, is that at the beginning of the 'eighties Bellini turned back to a tighter, more linear mode — stimulated, perhaps, by the nature of his subject.

II

In its most exceptional aspect — a lone figure embraced by an extended landscape — the Frick panel recalls the representations of another saint that first became popular in the Quattrocento — St. Jerome in the "wilderness." No other subject exemplifies more vividly the emergence within a religious context of the early Renaissance curiosity about the natural world and delight in its endlessly varied beauty. Most of the paintings of this theme are small, produced for private contemplation, and they offered to the sophisticated urban collectors models of a thoughtful life led apart from society in an orderly, bounteous suburb. Thus they anticipate the pastoral idyll that became prominent in the literature of the sixteenth century.

The theme of St. Jerome in the "wilderness," which brings man, animals and nature so inti-

[19]

mately together, was favored especially in Venice, indeed it became a Venetian theme *par excellence*.[36] Giovanni Bellini himself is chiefly responsible for its special development there. With more or less assistance from his workshop he painted the subject no less than four times. He made first the charming small panel in the Barber Institute, Birmingham (Fig. 37),[37] then the beautiful silvery predella of the Pesaro altarpiece (Fig. 36), the large picture in the Contini Collection (Fig. 34), and the panel in the National Gallery, Washington (dated 1505), in that order.[38] At least two other representations of the subject emanated from his circle, executed perhaps partly on his designs.[39] Finally, near the age of eighty in 1513, when painting for S. Giovanni Crisostomo, Bellini returned to the subject once again, permitting it to invade the upper space of an altarpiece given over to formal cult images.[40] These paintings of St. Jerome by Bellini share with the *St. Francis* broad aspects of theme and design and landscape. In them Bellini makes a characteristic innovation: to the rocky "desert" traditionally associated with the saint and still visible in the work of his father Jacopo, he adds, already in the very early Birmingham picture, a peaceful pastoral countryside. This grows in scope and gradually usurps the place of the "wilderness."

All these paintings share, too, similar wild and domesticated creatures. Predatory animals, such as the dragons, jackals and serpents with which Jacopo Bellini surrounded St. Jerome,[41] have no place in Giovanni's benign world. In his very early Birmingham panel a rabbit, frequent denizen of late medieval and early Renaissance landscapes, including Mantegna's,[42] emerges from his hole with a quizzical expression much like that of the rabbit in the Frick painting. In the field behind a horse is grazing, perhaps the "ass" guarded by Jerome's lion, according to the legend.[43] There are rabbits as well as birds, including a heron, in Carlo Crivelli's painting of St. Jerome in the National Gallery, London. Here again a horse — or is it a deer? — stands nearby (Fig. 35). A squirrel, some birds and a deer inhabit the landscape of Bellini's *St. Jerome* in the Contini Collection (Fig. 34), and similar creatures may be seen in a *St. Jerome* attributed to Cima in Harewood House.[44] In paintings of the Veneto and nearby the "wilderness" of St. John the Baptist contains similar inhabitants. A heron meditates alongside the saint in Garofalo's picture in the Fitzwilliam Museum, Cambridge (Fig. 38), possibly contemplating the extraordinary congregation nearby, consisting of a wild boar, an ostrich, a lion, two rabbits and a very sentimental bear.

The animals in the Frick panel are, then, the familiar companions of saints who live alone, apart from society. There are other familiar elements of the environment of such saints. The bell may be seen in, for instance, two paintings of St. Jerome by or close to Ercole de' Roberti.[45] Jerome is commonly barefoot, while his sandals are often displayed nearby,[46] and a simple wooden cross is stuck into the ground. In Bellini's *St. Jerome* in the Contini Collection (Fig. 34), the cross is like the one in the Frick *St. Francis*.[47] Crivelli's *St. Jerome* in London includes, in a rustic cell, a table (but not a lectern) and some books (Fig. 35). The skull in the Frick picture, on the other hand, is something of an innovation. As a symbol of mortality and an instrument of penitential contemplation it was introduced into representations of St. Jerome, as Janson has shown, only in the 'seventies.[48] Its connection with St. Francis seems to begin in the Frick panel.[49] It is a commonplace of later representations of the saint, whether devotional or historical (Stigmatization).[50]

In the light of all these relationships we might well conclude that the painting in the Frick

[20]

Collection simply represents St. Francis, like St. Jerome, "in the wilderness." This is precisely the title given it a few years after Bellini's death, for it was very probably the Frick painting that Marcantonio Michiel saw in 1525 in the house of Taddeo Contarini in Venice and which he described as follows:

"La tavola del S. Francesco nel deserto fu opera de Zuan Bellino cominciata da lui a M. Zuan Michiel, e ha un paese propinquo finito e ricercato mirabilmente." (The panel of St. Francis in the wilderness was the work of Giovanni Bellini, begun by him for Messer Zuan Michiel; and it has a landscape close by, admirably studied and worked out.)[51]

This succinct description gives little comfort to the secularists who claim that in its time the painting was understood as pure landscape, for Michiel identifies the religious subject first and refers to the landscape last, after recording the name of the painter and his client. In any event, the authority of an early opinion may be invoked to support what seems the simplest solution of the problem of interpretation. This solution however presents serious difficulties. There was, first of all, no tradition for the representation of St. Francis in the wilderness, whether praying, communing, or simply existing, and Bellini's painting, so far as I know, did not inaugurate one. It was only in the late sixteenth century that painters began to represent St. Francis out-of-doors in a state of religious ecstasy.[52] It is true that in the central panel of his Borgo Sansepolcro altarpiece Sassetta, following Taddeo di Bartolo, had painted St. Francis "in glory," his arms outstretched and his eyes turned to heaven.[53] This beautiful painting may even have been seen by Bellini, but in it the rapture occurs within the formal composition of a didactic cult image. The saint, placed frontally, tramples on personifications of the three great Franciscan vices. As an ecstatic St. Francis in an extended landscape, Bellini's painting would thus seem to be both unprecedented and unique until a much later time.

If then the Frick picture does not seem to portray the saint simply in a certain state of mind, it must represent a known experience in his life. But which? The small sheet of paper slipped below his girdle together with the fact that he addresses the heavens might suggest that he is engaged in composing, perhaps the Hymn to the Sun. The attitude of the saint is however not creative but receptive, and his gesture has this significance in other paintings of the time, as we have seen. Furthermore in all medieval and Renaissance art no such scene of poetic creation was ever portrayed, and, if it were, the saint would not appear in a mountain wilderness but seated in a hut near the monastery of S. Damiano, where the legends say the poem was composed.[54]

What then of the Stigmatization itself? While the landscape and the posture of the saint suggest it in a general way, some elements of the traditional representation are lacking. Neither Brother Leo nor the little chapel is represented. St. Francis is standing rather than kneeling, and he does not raise his arms and hands in the familiar manner. The wounds are not conspicuous; indeed two of them, one in a foot and the other in his side, are not visible at all. Most important of all, the seraph, central symbol of the event, fails to appear in the heavens. There are, it is true, representations of the Stigmatization that resemble Bellini's picture in one or another of these respects, but in no one work are all these unusual features combined. The wound in the side is lacking in almost all the very early representations,[55] and likewise in those in which the saint faces towards the left, as in the Frick panel (Fig. 1).[56] Neither Tommaso da Celano nor Bonaventura says that Francis was kneeling at the time of the Stigmatization, and the saint was occasionally shown standing in both Northern and Italian paintings of the Stigmatization.[57] Sometimes he assumes a position between standing and kneeling, notably in a Mantegnesque panel in the Gardner Museum, Boston (Fig. 51).[58] In Bartolommeo della Gatta this unstable posture, as we have seen, is combined with Bellini's gesture and other elements of Bellini's composition (Fig. 39), so that we seem to possess a painter's judgment in the 'eighties that the Frick panel represented the Stigmatization. In a few other representations too, one of which is earlier than the Frick panel (Fig. 27), the conventional position of the hands is replaced by a gesture that resembles somewhat the one in the Frick panel. And the rustic cell is occasionally introduced, particularly in one painting that follows closely the text of the *Sacre Sante Stimmate*.[59]

Apart from Bartolommeo della Gatta's important testimony, the unusual representations of the Stigmatization do no more than tell us that Bellini's picture might conceivably be one. We would therefore remain hesitant were not other aspects of the work no less compelling. The rocky setting, first of all, suggests La Verna, the mountain to which St. Francis retired shortly before the supernatural experience.

As Dante described it:

"nel crudo sasso intra Tevere ed Arno
da Cristo prese l'ultimo sigillo."[60]

Whereas Bellini's contemporaries in Florence, such as Domenico Ghirlandaio, portrayed this site in the distance and in much smaller scale than the saint in the foreground (Fig. 43), Giovanni in characteristic manner set the figure immediately below the crag. Furthermore the rocks that he painted show — as Howard Davis kindly pointed out to me — a remarkable resemblance to actual masses at La Verna (Fig. 41). The site itself was not distant from Bellini's presumed route to or from Pesaro, and if he went to Borgo and Arezzo, it lay quite near. We must moreover recall that the Frick painting was made during a period just after this trip when the painter was incorporating in his pictures monuments he had seen along the way.

Ghirlandaio's fresco is instructive in other ways too (Fig. 43). It shows that even in Florentine painting, where one would least expect them, wild animals inhabited the landscape of the Stigmatization. Already in Sienese painting of the thirteenth century, indeed, a few birds and mammals — often a bear — shared the countryside with Francis (Fig. 45). Two deer are prominent in Ghirlandaio's painting, and again (are they actually deer?) in Bartolommeo della Gatta's (Fig. 39). There is a deer also in representations of the Stigmatization by Jacopo Bellini and by Michele Giambono (Fig. 27).[61] In the latter the relationship of the stag to the scene as a whole is much the same as that of the donkey in Bellini's picture.

The kinds of animals and birds that inhabit the landscapes of the Stigmatization vary as much as those that appear alongside St. Jerome or the Baptist, so that they seem to be present as representatives of the wild creatures that accompany holy hermits and as manifestations of the Quattro-

[22]

cento love of the natural world. Whether in addition to these two categories of meaning they are endowed with a third and indeed a fourth — whether, in other words, as *specific creatures* they are connected with objects and events in the legend of the saint, and also symbolize more general religious concepts — is, as often, difficult to say. Perhaps we may recognize in the rabbit the leveret that St. Francis protected.[62] The ass is possibly the one that carried the saint up Mount Alverna.[63] Still, when proposing so specific an identity we must remember not only the stag in a similar position in portrayals of the Stigmatization but also the nearly identical ass, again standing quietly and alone, in a dooryard in the Niccolini *Crucifixion* (Fig. 60), and in the woods in the Bellinesque *Martyrdom of St. Peter Martyr* in London.[64] Perhaps the spring, which in Mantegna's *Agony in the Garden* in Tours (Fig. 24) and in other paintings may be a sort of *fons vitae*, alludes to the spring described in the *Sacre Sante Stimmate*, though that was not at the actual site of the Stigmatization.

But even after we have pointed to the legend of the saint, it is conceivable (I do not say probable) that we have not exhausted the religious meanings of the forms in the painting. In medieval thought the ass, for instance, can symbolize, in addition to many evil qualities, the people whom Christ leads to the heavenly kingdom.[65] The gray heron in Bellini's picture, which corresponds to the fowl in Giambono's (Fig. 27), can refer to the souls of the elect[66] or to ideas of righteousness[67] or penitence.[68] Such meanings can be attributed of course not only to the living creatures in the picture but to the plants also. The grapevine commonly signifies Christ's sacrifice, but then it usually bears fruit, as in Mantegna's *Agony* in Tours (Fig. 24), which Bellini certainly knew, so that its lack of grapes in the Frick panel is almost pointed.[69] The other plants may all be found in paintings by Bellini of a variety of subjects. The brambles appear again in the Contini *St. Jerome* (Fig. 34), and in it as well as the *St. Jerome* in Washington we may see an ivy vine and a fig tree. Ivy twines around a stump in the Naples *Transfiguration* (Fig. 62). Recently Klauner has pointed to the presence of ivy and fig in other paintings by Bellini — the *Man of Sorrows* in Stockholm and the *Descent into Limbo* in Bristol — as well as in compositions by many other masters of the late fifteenth and early sixteenth centuries, particularly of the Venetian region, and she has concluded that these plants are connected in meaning with a sequence of more or less related things and ideas, ranging from the tree of knowledge to the virtues of the saints and the birth and passion of Christ.[70]

The impressive laurel tree in Bellini's painting poses for us a more urgent, though no more soluble, problem of interpretation. In many earlier representations of the Stigmatization the saint stands before a cave,[71] and near him a tree seems to curl and twist in response to the intensity of his experience (Fig. 45).[72] The portrayal of an active tree seems to be rooted in the tradition of the Stigmatization. It is perhaps significant, however, that in Bellini's picture this tree has become a laurel — a *laurus nobilis*, whose very name suggests the values that it symbolized. Inasmuch as the laurel was believed to be resistant to fire, it designated enduring, indestructible virtues. In his *Reductorium Morale* Berchorius compared it with the cross, which kept mankind from the fire of eternal damnation.[73] Dealing with the story of Apollo and Daphne in his moralized Ovid, he said that the laurel signifies the crucifix, and that Apollo embraced the laurel tree as Christ the cross.[74] The applicability to St. Francis is obvious. This text of the mid-fourteenth century certainly circulated in north Italy,[75] but whether Bellini or someone in his circle was familiar with it we cannot say.

It is difficult to know whether the painter invested the objects in his picture with any of the meanings we have just discussed. Lacking specifically relevant texts, we can only evaluate the probabilities in the light of late Quattrocento painting in general, and Bellini's work, especially of this period, in particular. The exercise of these historical methods, "tempered, if possible, by common sense" (to use Erwin Panofsky's unforgettable phrase),[76] leaves the question undecided. In a panel painted by Bellini not long before the Frick picture, the *Man of Sorrows* in London, one of the reliefs behind Christ represents a pagan sacrifice, which his hand blots out, and the landscape behind seems differentiated or "moralized."[77] On Christ's left the structures are ruinous, and the large tree on the hill is bare of leaves. On his right the light is brighter, the world warmer, the buildings intact. In many other paintings however Bellini seems to ignore such connotations. In the Pesaro *St. Jerome*, for instance, some verdant trees are visible in the distance while a large dead tree, conspicuously rotting but indubitably picturesque, rises alongside the saint. There is a similar specimen on the Virgin's *right* in the *Assumption* in S. Pietro Martire, Murano.[78] Furthermore, in both the *Transfiguration* in Naples (Fig. 62) and the late *Pietà* in the Academy[79] a prominent bare tree appears on Christ's *right*, while a leafy one may be seen at his *left*.[80] A similar indifference either to the symbolism of position or to symbolic content itself may be observed in a panel in London, where on the Madonna's *right* a serpent attacks a crane.[81]

III

Bellini placed the large tree, traditional in the *Stigmatization*, at the left margin of his painting while locating the cave at the right, and they are given the same position in a painting of the subject by the workshop of Federigo Barocci in the Uffizi (Fig. 47).[82] This spirited picture, painted about a hundred years after Bellini's work, has evidently much in common with it. So similar indeed are the two that one wonders what might be the connection between them — whether both painters had in mind the same actual site, or whether Barocci had seen Bellini's picture.

Barocci placed the cleft in the rock immediately behind St. Francis, giving it a shape generally similar to his. Here as in numerous other paintings of the Stigmatization (Fig. 27) this form represents the depression in the rock described in the appendix to the *Fioretti* called *Considerazioni sulle Sacre Sante Stimmate*.[83] While St. Francis was living at La Verna before the Stigmatization, according to the text, he was attacked by the devil at a precipitous height. Unable to escape by any ordinary means, he was saved by a miraculous softening of the rock behind that, "like melted wax," permitted him to sink back into it. Thereafter the rock permanently retained the form of the saint. The cave at the far right in Bellini's picture, while somewhat similar in outline to the saint, serves as his cell and is provided with a gate so that it does not clearly allude to the event described in the *Considerazioni*. But what of the rock just behind him which, as we have already said, seems to have melted to accommodate his figure?

[24]

Barocci undoubtedly knew the *Considerazioni* because he put into the tree the falcon which, the text says, made a nest near the saint's cell and saw to it that he awakened early each morning for matins.[84] In Barocci's picture, as in the texts, the Stigmatization occurs at night, and the supernatural light emanating from the seraph falls upon the mountain. The *Actus*, a life of St. Francis written ca. 1325 that greatly influenced the *Fioretti*, says simply:

"Et apparuit (Christus in specie Seraph) cum tanto splendore de nocte quod illuminavit montes et valles circumquaque distinctos amplius quam si solis claritas affuisset. De quo testes fuerunt pastores qui per partes illas cum gregibus vigilabant."

"And at night Christ (in the form of a Seraph) appeared with such brilliance that he lighted the hills and valleys around more distinctly than if the brightness of the sun had fallen on them. Witnesses of this were some shepherds who were tending their sheep in the region."[85]

The *Considerazioni* is more elaborate and melodramatic and it adds a reference to the inns in the neighborhood and to some mule-drivers:

"In questa apparizione mirabile tutto il monte della Verna parea che ardesse di fiamma isplendidissima, la quale risplendeva e illuminava tutti i monti e le valli d'intorno, come se fusse il sole sopra la terra; onde i pastori che vegliavano in quelle contrade, veggendo il monte infiammato e tanta luce d'intorno, ebbono grandissima paura, secondo che eglino poi narrarono a' frati, affermando, che quella fiamma era durata sopra il monte della Verna per ispazio d'un'ora e più. Similmente allo splendore di questo lume, il quale risplendeva negli alberghi della contrada per le finestre, certi mulattieri, che andavano in Romagna, si levarono credendo che fusse levato il sole e sellarono e caricarono le bestie loro e camminando vidono il detto lume cessare, e levarsi il sole materiale."

"Then the whole mount of La Verna seemed to flame forth with dazzling splendor, that shone and illumined all the mountains and the valleys round about, as were the sun shining on the earth. Wherefore when the shepherds who were watching in that country saw the mountain aflame and so much brightness round about they were sore afraid, according as they afterwards told the friars, and affirmed that that flame had endured over the mount of La Verna for the space of an hour and more. Likewise, certain muleteers who were going to Romagna arose up at the brightness of this light which shone through the windows of the inns of that country, and thinking that the sun had risen, saddled and loaded their beasts. And as they went their way, they saw the said light wane and the real sun rise. . . ."[86]

In a meadow beyond the mountain in Barocci's painting we see two men illuminated by a camp-fire in the dooryard of a building (an inn?). One of them points out the miracle to the other.[87] Beyond the miraculous radiance and the dark night the dawn breaks, touching one cloud with a rosy glow.

These aspects of the Stigmatization described by the texts had occasionally been represented in art before the time of Barocci. Piero della Francesca in the predella of his Perugia altarpiece had already laid the event at night,[88] while other painters, though avoiding the nocturnal setting, included the incidents in the vicinity. At the extreme right in Ghirlandaio's fresco some riders have stopped their horses in midstream and are looking up at the heavens, in the general direction of the seraph (Fig. 43). One of them shields his eyes from the bright light. Behind St. Francis two friars look upward also, so that the painter has dealt freely with the account in the legends. Any

[25]

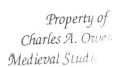

doubt that the texts lie behind these actions is removed by another example of the Stigmatization in the Pinacoteca at Modena (Fig. 46). This feeble work, Florentine of the late fifteenth century, was obviously influenced by Ghirlandaio's fresco. Yet it gives a conspicuous place in the landscape to a mule-driver (or is it not perhaps a donkey-driver?) who "as (he) went his way, saw the (strange) light wane and the real sun rise." The same person, with a beast of burden that likewise defies precise zoological classification, looks into the heavens in Lo Spagna's fresco in the Municipio, Narni.[89]

In the light of these texts and paintings some aspects of Bellini's landscape immediately attract our attention. Within the burg lying in the sunlight in the distance not a person or an animal is visible (Fig. 8). Unlike the towns in other works by the painter, such as the Niccolini *Crucifixion* (Fig. 60), it is entirely empty, as it would be at night. In the green meadow stretching out before it, amidst a flock of sheep, stands a shepherd leaning on his crook and looking intently in the general direction of the saint. Now there is a similar shepherd leaning on his crook in the *Resurrection*, but he looks off to the right, away from the action of the painting (Fig. 33). The shepherd in the *Madonna in a Meadow* in London, like the one in the Frick panel, looks in the direction of the beholder, but he is lying casually in the grass.[90] A shepherd relaxes similarly in the *Madonna* of 1510 in the Brera,[91] and he has fallen asleep in the *Assumption* in S. Pietro Martire, Murano[92] — another of the sleeping figures that, as I have pointed out elsewhere, appear in the tranquil art of the Venetians.[93] Sometimes the shepherd drives along a flock of sheep or some cattle, as in the *Transfiguration* (Fig. 62) or the Uffizi allegory.[94] In all these paintings he is present as the inhabitant of a rich productive countryside, and he conveys the poetry of a life in close relation to nature. Only in the Frick panel does he seem engrossed with a religious event. Could he be one of those shepherds who, according to the legends, were witnesses of the miracle of Monte Alverna?

What the shepherds saw, according to the legends, was the sudden brightness of the mountain at night, and although in the picture no nocturnal illumination of this sort seems at first to be portrayed, there is in one part of it a very strange luminary phenomenon. Most of the painting is lighted in a quite normal way — normal, that is, for the Quattrocento and more particularly for Bellini in the later 'seventies. In works of this period beginning with the Pesaro *Coronation*, space for the first time seems filled with light. In the Frick panel as in the Berlin *Resurrection* (Fig. 33) that immediately preceded it this light has a definite source, and certain prominent forms relatively near the beholder cast shadows on the ground. In the Frick panel this is true of the saint, the arbor, the lectern, and the donkey. The angle of all of these shadows is approximately the same, indicating that the source of the light is at the left just a little in front of the plane of the picture. With the exception of the donkey's these shadows are all long, and the full light penetrates to the further cross-bar of the lower part of the lectern (Fig. 15). Here as in all Bellini's early work the source of the light is rather low.

The light falls full on the saint, who is turned at right angles to it. Though he looks a little above it, one has the impression that his experience is somehow bound up with it. To a degree there is nothing unusual about this. The association of light with spirituality is as old as religion itself, and earlier in the Quattrocento, in Fra Filippo's *Vision of St. Augustine* in the Uffizi, for instance, this

[26]

association had been made vivid and central in pictorial representations. But whereas in Fra Filippo's painting a supernatural figure may be seen within the radiance, in Bellini's work there is nothing but the light itself. We have observed that in paintings up to Bellini's time the seraph is, with the rarest exceptions, a central form in the representation of the Stigmatization.[95] No such figure is visible in the Frick panel. X-rays do not show that one was ever planned, and although the panel was originally slightly higher, it is unlikely that one existed in the missing section.[96]

The quality of the light in the painting that we have already described is not in itself unusual, but in the sky in the upper left-hand corner of the painting, deeper in space than the main source of light, there is a remarkable occurrence (Fig. 21).[97] Not far above the horizon the clouds seem to part, revealing an intense radiance. Yellow light radiates from these openings, tinging the edges of several clouds, and streaking across others. The rays disappear behind the tree, but on the other side of it the clouds are tinted yellow by them, and the distant landscape is bathed in a golden light.

It is clear that this luminary display is related to those earlier Quattrocento celestial phenomena that accompany the appearance of a supernatural figure. These phenomena are developed especially in the Netherlands, by Roger van der Weyden[98] and by Dirk Bouts (Fig. 50). Only a few years after Bellini another Italian painter, Filippino Lippi, who was equally fascinated by Netherlandish painting, introduced a similar, though more natural "glory" into his celebrated panel of the Virgin appearing to St. Bernard, in the Badia, Florence. And Bellini's pupil, Titian, lighted the sky of his early *Madonna* in London (no. 635) with similar yellow rays, to suggest the miracle of the Incarnation and the appearance of the angel to the shepherds.

On closer examination of Bellini's painting it becomes evident that this phenomenon, unlike the others, has no clear natural basis. The clouds are not dense, as one would expect in an occurrence of this sort. They are in fact much less dense than the cumulous ones further to the right, and they are not visible everywhere around the radiance, so that in places it is the blue sky itself that seems to open. The yellow openings moreover are painted in a heavy impasto that is unique in the picture.[99] The concentration of forces in this region is increased by the location nearby of the pictorial point of sight. Does this unnatural illumination suggest the glory around the seraph — the sort of glory that had become increasingly naturalistic during the Quattrocento? Would it be a distant symbol of an unseen supernatural presence?

We must ask, in addition, a more difficult question. The light that streams into the foreground seems at first quite natural. It does, however, illuminate the rapt St. Francis, whose experience seems affected by it. The distant, unnatural light on the other hand seems to affect the movement of the laurel tree that rises in the foreground. Its branches, like the radiance above it, curl into an arc, and they seem stirred and pulled towards it, as by a magnetic force. Thus the two sources of light, although not realistically linked in space, seem related in their purpose and influence. Did Bellini therefore intend the entire space to be supernaturally lighted at night? When we recall the empty town and the watchful shepherd we are all the more impelled to wonder whether we do not witness precisely what was described by the texts, "the splendor that shone and illumined all the mountains and valleys round about, as were the sun shining on the earth."

I V

We are confronted with a mystery. Perhaps the nature of other paintings by Bellini will enable us to penetrate it, and will help us to decide whether in the Frick panel he might have taken the bold step of omitting a seraph from a Stigmatization. A few years before this work Bellini had, in fact, painted the same subject. In this panel, part of the predella of the Pesaro altarpiece (Fig. 40), all the traditional elements are included — the mountain, the seraph with a cross, the chapel (grown however to a large church), the reading friar, and even rudimentary rays that dart for a short distance from each wound. Despite these traditional forms the scene is in one respect most unusual. In early paintings of the Stigmatization the seraph hovers near the saint. During the Quattrocento, as a consequence of the development of perspective and of the desire to differentiate more decisively between the natural and the supernatural, the seraph often appeared deep in space, at a great distance from the saint. It was given this position in Domenico Veneziano's painting in Washington, and in a drawing in Jacopo Bellini's London "sketch book," which in this and some other respects resembles the Pesaro composition.[100] But in these earlier works the saint kneels either in profile or turned away from the beholder, looking at a seraph that hovers more or less deep in space. Giovanni Bellini's saint on the other hand faces outwards and the tiny seraph is at first scarcely visible, so that the saint seems moved by some purely internal vision. It is his ecstasy alone with which the beholder is confronted.

The painter's desire to dwell exclusively on the spiritual experience of the saint has other consequences, too. His novel posture near frontality entails an exceptional position for the seraph. However it may be visible to the saint, the beholder sees it only from behind. The seraph is reversed also in Marco Zoppo's *Stigmatization* in the Walters Gallery, Baltimore, though its apparent size is far greater (Fig. 42). If Zoppo's seraph derives from Bellini's, as seems quite likely, we have new evidence for the date of the Pesaro altarpiece, because Zoppo's panel was probably part of the altarpiece he painted (for Pesaro also) in 1471. This question is discussed in an appendix.

Bellini carried the startling visual diminution of the heavenly figure further by imbedding it, so to speak, in the architecture of the great church behind. The arm of the cross is exactly parallel to the gable immediately below it, and the entire form seems at first to be attached to the roof, like some gigantic gargoyle.[101] But we really cannot be sure that the seraph is near the church at all. If the glance of the saint and the rays issuing from his wounds are directed towards it, it must on the contrary hover very near the picture plane. For this place, however, it is far too small. If on the other hand it is near the church, then its back is turned to the saint as well as to the beholder. We can only conclude that the painter, concerned with the inner excitement of the saint, was quite content with the ambiguity of the seraph's position. The relevance of this spatial ambiguity to the luminary ambiguity in the Frick panel is evident.

The unnatural event in the Pesaro *Stigmatization* is not reflected in the sky, which is normal and serene. In another predella of this altarpiece, however — the *Conversion of St. Paul* — Christ appears before a yellow light. The sky to the right of him is darkened by swirling clouds and the horizon is streaked in red.

[28]

While the Pesaro *Stigmatization* anticipates the painting in the Frick Collection by reducing the evidence of the supernatural and implying a more immanent religion, several other panels made by Bellini around this time manifest more clearly the new spiritual connotations of nature.

The *Agony in the Garden* in London was painted around 1460, early in the master's career (Fig. 44). One of his greatest and, in a sense, most revolutionary works, it is concerned with a subject much like the Stigmatization – a vision of a heavenly figure who brings a final prophecy of Passion and death. The style of the painting is Mantegnesque and, as is well known, Bellini followed in many respects Mantegna's composition of the same subject also now in London.[102] In this work Christ is approached by a bevy of angels, actually winged putti, standing on a cloud and bearing symbols of the Passion. Bellini reduced the number of angels to one, and even this one is denied the substantiality that such figures had traditionally possessed.

Angels, though originally conceived as emanations of God and thus as pure spirit, were early in Christian poetry and art given a body. They were normally endowed with the same substance as other figures. Theologians, however, adhering to the conception of angels as spiritual essences, often compared them with light.[103] In late medieval art angels are sometimes portrayed as *sources* of light; they radiated it, as in Taddeo Gaddi's *Annunciation to the Shepherds* in S. Croce, Florence. In a *Gethsemane* from the circle of Taddeo di Bartolo in the museum at Copenhagen the entire angel, including the flesh surfaces, is opaque white.[104] But a more fundamental association with light is adumbrated in other representations, where the angels begin to lose substance and become immaterial like light itself. In Ambrogio Lorenzetti's *Madonna* in the Pinacoteca, Siena, their heads are rendered in his normal mode, but their bodies are painted over the incised rays emanating from the Virgin, so that they acquire a diaphanous character (Fig. 52). In the circle of Fra Angelico angels are frequently rendered by a network of white lines on a blue sky.[105] The unearthly nature of saints is sometimes represented in a similar manner. In the panel of the rescue of the three maidens in the Uffizi Ambrogio Lorenzetti painted St. Nicholas in pale gray and blue over gold leaf so that, unlike the other figures, the saint is almost translucent. Occasionally the Byzantine method of striation in gold is revived for this purpose, as in the ascending body of St. Francis in the Bolognese panel of his *Death* in the Vatican Gallery.[106]

In Bellini's figure in London the dematerialization is more complete (Fig. 49). His angel belongs to a different order of reality than the other figures in the painting: it is a white, nearly weightless, translucent spirit. Such a spirit has no need of a substantial supporting cloud, but Bellini felt that it still needed something, and he put into the distant sky a cloud that, though far behind the figure, provides a sort of cushion for its feet. Christ in the Berlin *Resurrection* is provided with a similar distant support (Fig. 33).

Ghostly angels like Bellini's soon began to appear in the work of other painters under his influence, as Foppa's *Martyrdom of St. Sebastian* in Villa I Tatti, Florence,[107] or Ercole de' Roberti's *Agony in the Garden* in Dresden (Fig. 48). These pallid figures are "present" in the representation only in a special sense, and they readily acquire a private character, as though seen only by one of the actors or the beholder of the painting. We cannot always be certain, in fact, just what they represent, whether miraculous appearances or the images in an actor's mind. Forms approximating these may be seen in Ercole's extraordinary *Vesperbild* in Liverpool. Behind the Virgin bearing her dead son in her lap Christ appears again, in a strange sort of filmy Crucifixion (Fig. 53). This panel stood at the center of a predella between two long panels now in Dresden, one representing the Agony in the Garden, to which we have just referred (Fig. 48), and the Betrayal, the other the Way to Calvary. The Crucifixion would then be an appropriate subject for the central panel. It is, however, not only relegated to the background but rendered more faintly than aerial perspective would seem to require, and indeed the figures, though bearing some color, are more diaphanous than those at an equal depth in the two predellas at the sides. Ercole's model, Tura's *Vesperbild* in the Correr, Venice (Fig. 55), makes no such distinctions, and they were not understood by Mazzolino when he took the figure of Christ into his panel now in the Cini Collection.[108] Ercole's intention apparently transcended the observance of naturalistic principles, and this is indicated also by the relative sketchiness of the entire setting, including the foreground, compared to the two main figures. The painter seems to suggest not a present event but a past one, a memory that haunts the mind of the Virgin and of the beholder.

In medieval art the content of the mind's eye or of conversation was portrayed in the same mode as the figures themselves.[109] In the representation, for instance, of Pharaoh's dream in the late thirteenth-century mosaic in the Baptistery, Florence, the cattle and the sheaves of wheat are no less substantial than the dreamer (Fig. 57). The rise of naturalism in the fourteenth and fifteenth centuries created the conditions for a differentiation. A mode of shimmering, ghostly forms, related to those we have described, was introduced earlier in the fifteenth century to represent a vision. In a miniature in the *Bedford Hours*, for instance, the premonitions of the Passion that assailed Christ as he knelt alone in the Garden of Olives actually hover, as pallid images, over his head (Fig. 54). These ghostly figures were no doubt influenced by the indistinct bluish forms that are visible in the backgrounds of fifteenth-century landscapes — forms that are, in short, affected by aerial perspective. Thus one of the great triumphs of naturalism is subverted to unnatural ends. The method of portraying the spatially distant is utilized for the psychologically hidden and the metaphysical.

It is evident that Bellini's study of light and color during the 'sixties and 'seventies had important consequences for his iconography and his meaning as well as for his "form."[110] In the *Man of Sorrows* in London, furthermore, the quality of the light is essential in differentiating the cool, gray, ruinous Old World from the warm, productive New, as I have suggested elsewhere.[111] In the *Gethsemane* in London it is not only the ghostly angel that was made possible by Bellini's researches (Fig. 44). The spirituality of the moment is of course conveyed by the communication between Christ and the angel holding the chalice, but it is extended and deepened by the marvelous quality of the landscape and, even more, the light that fills it. The lower part of the sky is bright with a radiance that issues from an invisible sun. The head of Christ, rising above the horizon into this area, has a sort of immense natural halo. Or shall we, on the contrary, judge that the ardor of Christ has lighted the world and the sky? There is here the fullest union of human experience, natural phenomenon and supernatural event. Bellini has indeed insisted on this identity by placing just below the luminous angel a tower that is similarly vertical in shape and set out

[30]

against the blue sky. It glows with the light of the sun, and it constitutes a sort of complement in the natural world to the human and heavenly forms that are near it.

Two paintings by Bellini of the Transfiguration are also relevant to our theme (Figs. 61, 62). Again the subject is similar — a figure transported by a vision. When representing this event Quattrocento painters such as Baldovinetti had already abandoned the symbolic *mandorla* that once surrounded Christ.[112] Bellini, in his very early representation in the Museo Correr, preserved only a narrow band of parallel rays around Christ, but above him he introduced a new form (Fig. 61). In the sky is visible a large circle of white clouds almost, but not quite, normal in appearance. This slightly unnatural ring alludes, no doubt, to the "bright cloud" that "overshadowed" Christ and the prophets, and out of which came "a voice . . . saying, This is my beloved Son. . . . "[113] Down below James sleeps — a characteristic Venetian innovation[114] — and John looks poignantly in the direction of a tender shoot growing from the stump of an old tree that had been felled with an axe. Already here in a very early work a tree seems to assume an expressive and symbolic role something like that of the laurel in the Frick panel.

In the Pesaro altarpiece the drama of the conversion of St. Paul had already been echoed by a turbulent sky.[115] In the *Transfiguration* in Naples the spiritual excitement of Christ, who is outwardly calm and majestic, is conveyed by an agitation in the world around him (Fig. 62). The terrain consists of restlessly heaving, intersecting knolls, and in the sky behind Christ there are dancing masses of clouds. Just as in the Frick picture, moreover, the painter has injected into this entirely naturalistic context a novel, partly unnatural heavenly light, unseen by the figures in the painting. Though the brightest sky, nearest the sun, is at the left, numerous rays dart from the cloud immediately above the head of Christ.

These paintings by Bellini in London, Pesaro and Naples, made around the time of the Frick panel, give us good reason to suppose that the painter, wishing to dwell on the religious exaltation of St. Francis, took the bold step of symbolizing a supernatural power in a Stigmatization not by a seraph but by a partly natural, partly unnatural radiation in the sky. Such a fundamental transformation of the theme was already prepared in the Pesaro altarpiece (Fig. 40), and it would not have remained unique in the history of the representation of the subject. Later Renaissance and baroque paintings tended increasingly to give to light a metaphysical function, and the seraph was often replaced by the tiny head of an angel.[116] Furthermore, in a fresco in the vault of a chapel in the Palazzo Vecchio, Florence — a fresco that no doubt represents the Stigmatization because of the behavior of Francis and Brother Leo — Bronzino has referred to the supernatural essence by a radiance alone (Fig. 56).[117] The pictorial field, it is true, is unusually constricted. The center of the vault, now occupied by the Trinity, originally showed only the donor's arms. A generation or so later painters such as Moretto in, broadly speaking, the Bellinesque tradition, limited the heavenly phenomena in the Conversion of St. Paul to a shaft of light and eliminated the traditional image of God, though in this subject, it is true, his presence was not required by the texts (Fig. 58).[118] Finally, Orazio Gentileschi or a painter close to him represented St. Francis kneeling on a rock outside a cave, his arms flung out and his wounds prominent. He is overwhelmed by a light in which there is no trace of the explicitly supernatural (Fig. 59).

All the natural light that Bellini paints so lovingly is transformed in the religious context. More than any earlier Italian painter he invested light with varying shades of spiritual significance, ranging from a general transfiguration of the natural world to a more explicit supernatural symbolism. His work in the 'sixties and 'seventies thus marks a major stage in one of the main currents of Renaissance painting. Masters in the early fifteenth century — Gentile, Masaccio, not to mention the Northerners — began to endow light with a basic expressive function. No doubt these ventures were inspired to a degree by the enduring theological association of light and the divine. But of course painters were observing with unprecedented intensity the world around them. They became fascinated with light before the humanists, led by Ficino, fell under the spell of Neoplatonism. This philosophy, which conveys some of its central tenets by similes and metaphors of radiance, affected greatly the course of painting. But there is another aspect of the relationship. Ficino's principal work was done in the same decades as the painting of Bellini that we have considered. The luminous philosophy and the luminous art are parallel phenomena. Indeed, when considering the rise of Neoplatonism in the Quattrocento we may wonder whether painting, which later received so much from it, did not earlier, through its luminous imagery, contribute something to it.

Bellini's modification of the Stigmatization would probably have been facilitated by the fact that the painting, unlike his other large panels, was made for a private person. "Cominciata da lui a M. Zuan Michiel," said Marcantonio Michiel; and Messer Zuan, even if he did not welcome so personal a religious conception, would very probably have permitted the painter greater iconographic freedom than any official body. We know in fact that one of the greatest patrons in Italy could not induce Bellini, at least in his later years, to provide what he did not feel inclined to paint. From 1496 to 1505 Isabella d'Este tried every available means to obtain from the master a mythological painting for her *studiolo* in Mantua to set alongside those painted by Mantegna and, later, other masters. She first had to retreat from a fixed subject to something vaguely antique — "cosa antiqua e de bello significato" — and then, eight years later, she was obliged to accept simply a Madonna and Child with the youthful Baptist. In it, moreover, Bellini exerted himself not so much for his demanding patroness but, we are told, chiefly out of respect for the Gonzaga painter — "massime per respecto de Andrea Mantegna." Isabella pressed Bellini again in 1504–05 for a painting for her *studiolo* and asked her representative, the writer Pietro Bembo, to choose a subject. After talking with Bellini he warned her that the "invenzione" must be left to the painter's imagination ("accomodata alla sua fantasia"). The painter liked to work, Bembo added, without fixed prescriptions ("signati termini"); indeed, he said to Bembo that he was accustomed to roam at will in his paintings — "sempre vagare a sua voglia nelle pitture."[119]

This phrase, which has a Giorgionesque ring, was, to be sure, formulated in 1506, with reference to a mythological subject. But Bellini had certainly begun to develop earlier the artistic independence and the freedom of imagination that it implies. Indeed his failure to stick to tradition, texts, or prescriptions is probably in part responsible for the elusiveness of the meaning of some elements of his allegories in the Uffizi or the Academy in Venice. These paintings were made within ten or twelve years of the *St. Francis*, and their subjects are Christian rather than antique.

[32]

Bellini preceded his pupil Giorgione in the formation of a new attitude toward creativity, and it is not improbable that when executing his panel for Zuan Michiel he found reason to "vagare nella pittura." The painting may thus be regarded as a precursor of *The Tempest*.

In the case of the Frick *St. Francis* iconographic freedom apparently involved, as it not infrequently does, a recapture of an old, largely forgotten, religious conception. From about the mid-thirteenth century on up to Bellini's time religious texts and paintings that dealt with the Stigmatization stressed increasingly the imprinting of the wounds on the body of St. Francis.[120] Painters introduced rays that pass from the wounds of Christ to those of the saint, and in the texts there was a related development until in the late (c. 1390) Franciscan treatise, *Liber de Conformitate Vitae b. Patris Francisci ad Vitam Nostri Jesu Christi* by Bartolommeo of Pisa, the visionary Christ actually printed the wounds with his own hands.[121] Such conceptions, however, were foreign to the period immediately following the death of the saint. As I have said elsewhere, "the early paintings of the Stigmatization in Italy and the north" (and the early texts also) "express the spiritual relation of Francis to God rather than his physical likeness to Christ incarnate."[122] Rays did not pass from wound to wound, and the broken body was subordinate to the communion with God. According to the earliest accounts, the signs of the stigmata were not actually visible until after the saint's death.[123] Even the relatively late *Fioretti* asserts that Francis was transformed into the likeness of Christ "non per martirio corporale ma per incendio mentale,"[124] and it is spiritual ardor that holds the saint rapt in the Frick painting. An unseen power, symbolized by the light, regenerates the saint and, so it seems, the whole of the visible world too — the wild-flowers and vine sprouting from the rocks, the dry branches bursting into leaf, and the quiet lonely donkey, who is mysteriously touched with life like Adam at the creation.

This power probably also is imprinting stigmata on the saint's body, though we cannot be absolutely sure. In this instance it is not the very end of the journey that is most interesting or even important, but what one could see along the way.

Giovanni Bellini, *St. Francis*. Detail. Landscape at upper left.

ST. FRANCIS OF ASSISI
CHRONOLOGY

1182	Born in Assisi, the son of a merchant.
1202	Captured and imprisoned in conflict between burghers and feudal nobility.
c. 1206	Began religious life and repaired Church of S. Damiano.
1209	Followers began to gather around St. Francis.
1209–10	Verbal approval of the Franciscan Rule by Pope Innocent III.
1223	Rule of the Order confirmed by Pope Honorius III.
1224	Stigmatization at La Verna.
1226	Death.
1228	Canonization.

GIOVANNI BELLINI

A NOTE ON HIS LIFE AND WORK

Solid facts about the first thirty years of Giovanni Bellini's career are exceedingly scarce. Of the greatest painter in Italy during this period — except for Leonardo da Vinci — we possess not one firmly dated work. Some evidence about his activity we have, and a long series of beautiful paintings, but the two categories do not clearly coincide. The case of Bellini is an extreme one in advanced Renaissance painting, and the fact that the debate about chronology, as the preceding essay shows, is normally reduced to limits of five rather than fifteen years is an indication that historians have got on with their job.

We first hear of the painter Giovanni Bellini in Venice in 1459, and in 1460 he added his name after that of his father Jacopo and his brother Gentile to an altarpiece in Padua, now lost. The first extant dated painting, which is also signed, is the *Madonna of the Trees* of 1487 in the Academy in Venice, but its condition is not good. By this time Giovanni Bellini had been working as an independent master for more than thirty years. His part in the four triptychs painted for the church of the Carità in Venice between 1462 and 1464 and now in the Academy is not easily extricated from that of collaborators. We see his own style of this early period undiluted in a series of Madonnas, of which the most superb perhaps are in the Museo Civico in Venice and the Accademia Carrara, Bergamo, followed a little later by the *Greek Madonna* in the Brera. Two outstanding Madonnas of this time are in American collections: the *Davis Madonna*, much damaged, in the Metropolitan Museum, and the panel in the Lehman Collection, New York. During these years Bellini frequently painted the Man of Sorrows also; unforgettable examples are in the Brera and the Poldi-Pezzoli Gallery in Milan. Other early works, the *St. Jerome* in Birmingham, the *Transfiguration* in the Museo Civico, Venice, and the wonderful *Agony in the Garden* in the National Gallery in London, have been discussed in the preceding text.

Historians have varied in their estimate of the value of two dates as guides to Bellini's painting in the seventies. In the eighteenth century 1472 was read on the much-damaged *Man of Sorrows* in the Ducal Palace, and forty years ago 1474 appeared on the back of the Fugger portrait in the Contini Collection, Florence. There is now general agreement that the *Resurrection* in Berlin, discussed in the preceding text, was finished by 1479. At this time Giovanni took over from his brother Gentile direction of a great civic enterprise, the historical paintings in the Ducal Palace, now entirely lost. With numerous assistants he worked there for many years.

[37]

From the late 'eighties on, a series of major dated altarpieces survives. The *S. Giobbe Madonna*, in the Academy, Venice, was probably painted before the *Madonna of the Trees*. From the year 1488 there are the famous triptych in the church of the Frari, Venice, and the *Madonna of Doge Barbarigo* in S. Pietro Martire, Murano. The *Baptism* in Santa Corona, Vicenza, between 1500 and 1502, shows a larger participation of assistants, while the majestic *Madonna and Saints* in S. Zaccaria, Venice, of 1505, is one of the great paintings of the early sixteenth century in Italy. The *St. Jerome* from Bellini's workshop in the Kress Collection, National Gallery, Washington, mentioned in the preceding text, is dated in the same year. During these years we are able to follow the master's continuous growth in a series of dated works, up to the splendid *Feast of the Gods* in the National Gallery, Washington. This painting, altered somewhat by Titian, was completed by Bellini in 1514, two years before his death.

Giovanni Bellini is thus represented exceptionally well in the United States. The greatness of the *St. Francis* among the relatively early works has never seriously been questioned, and the *Feast of the Gods* is a masterpiece of the last years. This representation is especially significant because of the wide range of the painter's art. He is the only leading Italian master, except perhaps the lesser Perugino, who began in an "Early Renaissance" phase, a style characteristic of the third quarter of the fifteenth century, and then developed a manner remarkably close to what we call "High Renaissance."

Despite Bellini's great historical importance and the rare beauty of his art his reputation did not survive as well as that of some contemporaries, Mantegna for instance, in centuries swayed by the Florentine-Roman tradition. His unique eminence in Venice and his tremendous superiority over Gentile Bellini were not clearly recognized until our time. In his own day, however, both his city and great private patrons such as Zuan Michiel and Isabella d'Este vied, as we have seen, for his services. When Albrecht Dürer returned to Venice late in 1505 he wrote that old Giovanni Bellini was "still the best in the art of painting." And on the day Bellini died in 1516 a fellow-Venetian wrote in his diary: "It is said that this morning Giovanni Bellini died, an excellent painter whose reputation is high throughout the world; and old though he was, he worked wonderfully."

SELECTIVE BIBLIOGRAPHY

HISTORY OF ART

Berenson, B., *Venetian Painting in America*, New York, 1916.

Brandi, C., "The Cleaning of Pictures in Relation to Patina, Varnish, and Glazes," *Burlington Magazine*, XCI, 1947, pp. 183–88.

Catalogue of the Frick Collection, Pittsburgh, I, 1949.

Dussler, L., *Giovanni Bellini*, Vienna, 1949.

Golubew, V., *Die Skizzenbücher Jacopo Bellinis*, Brussels, 1912.

Hartt, F., "Carpaccio's *Meditation on the Passion*," *Art Bulletin*, XXII, 1940, pp. 25–35.

Heinemann, F., *Giovanni Bellini e i Belliniani*, Venice, 1962.

Hendy, P., *Giovanni Bellini*, London, 1945.

Longhi, R., "Giovanni Bellini in Venice," *Burlington Magazine*, XCI, 1949, pp. 274 ff.

Mather, F. J., Jr., *Venetian Painters*, New York, 1936.

Meiss, M., "Jan van Eyck and the Italian Renaissance," in *Venezia e l'Europa, Atti del XVIII Congresso Internazionale di Storia dell' Arte*, Venice, 1956, pp. 58–69.

Michiel, Marc Antonio, *Notizie d'opere di disegno nella prima metà del secolo XVI*, ed. T. Frimmel, Vienna, 1888.

Pallucchini, R., *Catalogo della Mostra di Giovanni Bellini*, Venice, 1949.

——————, *Giovanni Bellini*, Milan, 1959.

Robertson, G., "The Earlier Work of Giovanni Bellini," *Journal of the Warburg and Courtauld Institutes*, XXIII, 1960, pp. 45–59.

ST. FRANCIS AND FRANCISCAN THOUGHT

Actus B. Francisci et Sociorum Eius, ed. P. Sabatier, Paris, 1902.

Facchinetti, P. V., *San Francesco d'Assisi*, Milan, 1921.

I Fioretti di San Francesco, ed. F. Casolini, Milan, 1926.

The Little Flowers of St. Francis (Everyman's Library), London and New York, 1951.

Moorman, J. R. H., *Sources for the Life of St. Francis*, Manchester, 1940.

Sabatier, P., *Vie de St. François d'Assise*, Paris, 1894.

APPENDIX
BELLINI, ZOPPO AND THE
PESARO ALTARPIECE

T<small>HE</small> *Stigmatization* by Marco Zoppo in the Walters Art Gallery probably formed part of the predella of this master's large altarpiece painted for the Minorities in Pesaro, as Mr. Berenson briefly suggested many years ago (Figs. 42, 63).[125] Zoppo's altarpiece, formerly in the Kaiser Friedrich Museum but burnt at the end of the Second World War, is 262 cm. high by 254 cm. wide.[126] The Walters panel measures 36 cm. high by 47 cm. wide.[127] Its height, a little more than one-eighth that of the panel once in Berlin, is thus within proper limits for a predella. If it were placed below the St. Francis, there would be space for a similar panel below each of the other saints as well as a longer one, more than one and a half the width of the others, beneath the Madonna.

Though the *Stigmatization* is not as well preserved as the large panel was, it seems to have been painted at the same moment in Zoppo's career. St. Francis is a younger man in the predella than in the large panel, but the design of his drapery is closely related. Especially striking is the geological similarity; the same swirling rocks, fantastic reformations of Mantegna's, appear in both panels. The halo of Francis, a translucent plate marked by diverging rays, is repeated in the large panel. If the church in the background of the Walters panel is, as Berenson suggested, a recollection of S. Ciriaco, Ancona — which seems probable — the ties of the *Stigmatization* with Zoppo's Pesaro altarpiece are increased. It is true that the altarpiece was signed "IN VINEXIA." It is true also that none of the descriptions of it, beginning with Vasari, mentions a predella,[128] but since the altarpiece had, by 1550, already been moved from one church to another, the predella might have been detached. Altogether the evidence is sufficient to attach the *Stigmatization* to the altarpiece with great probability.[129]

Inasmuch as Zoppo's altarpiece is dated 1471, the *Stigmatization* in Baltimore, if it belonged to it, would seem to provide evidence for the date of Giovanni Bellini's great work for the same city. Indeed, Bellini's altarpiece would seem to have been made for the same order, because though it has been connected with the church of S. Giovanni Battista in Pesaro,[130] the Baptist does not appear in the painting. The altarpiece went to the Museo Civico from S. Francesco, and St. Francis, though not (as in Zoppo's altarpiece) in the place of honor, is one of the four saints represented in the large panel. Bellini's altarpiece, which measures 262 x 240 cm. overall, is approximately as large as Zoppo's.

[41]

The representations of the Stigmatization by Bellini and Zoppo appear to be connected in some way. They share not only the novel averted seraph but broad similarities of composition (Figs. 40, 42). In both there is at one side a large rock mass with a cave, at the other side an exceptionally large church, and in between a battlemented city wall. There the resemblances seem to cease. In Zoppo's panel the seraph is much nearer to the saint and the posture of St. Francis is more conventional. Indeed Bellini's painting is in most respects much farther from the traditional composition, so that we must suppose either that it represents a development of Zoppo's composition, or that Zoppo reduced to more conventional terms a strikingly novel conception by Bellini. The former alternative would be in accord with the current estimate of the date of the Pesaro altarpiece, ca. 1473–75, and it would lead us to conclude that Bellini saw Zoppo's altarpiece either in Venice or in Pesaro when he arrived to undertake his own. The second alternative has however the great advantage of supposing that Bellini, rather than the less imaginative Zoppo, was the inventor of the averted seraph, and it therefore seems preferable. Of course there is the usual third possibility: the two paintings derive from a lost model. In the circumstances such a model is likely to have been the work only of Jacopo Bellini, Donatello in Padua, or Andrea Mantegna. No representations of the subject by Mantegna or Donatello have come down to us, and the two drawings by Jacopo Bellini show only a rather distant seraph, not an averted one.[131]

The upshot of all this is that Zoppo may have seen drawings for Bellini's Pesaro altarpiece, or even the altarpiece itself, before completing his in 1471. If he did, then Bellini's great work would have been under way a few years earlier than has usually, for stylistic reasons, been supposed. An earlier date, 1470–1472, would, furthermore, seem more plausible if the altarpiece, with its oddly prominent view of a castle, celebrated the capture of the Rocca di Gradara. This event, as we have mentioned above, occurred in 1463.[132]

Recently Prof. Pallucchini has proposed a similar relationship between the main fields of the altarpieces, and has therefore dated Bellini's around 1470.[133] Zoppo's combination of figures and landscape may reflect Bellini's, as Pallucchini has argued. The possibility of a connection seems clearest in the motif of landscape seen through the festoon. The pale, very distant mountains, furthermore, reflect Bellini, and they are therefore a departure from the canon, otherwise Mantegnesque, of the altarpiece. For a model of an altarpiece consisting of one large field, however, Zoppo would not have been dependent upon Bellini's Pesaro work, as Pallucchini says. Already in 1446 Antonio Vivarini, in his large Accademia altarpiece,[134] had abandoned the polyptych for a unified field. The rectangular punctures in the enclosing wall in this altarpiece, which open a view onto a woods behind, may perhaps have proved suggestive to Bellini when he was designing his panel for Pesaro.

NOTES TO THE TEXT

1 *Civilization of the Renaissance*, Part IV.
Most of the main ideas in this essay were presented in a lecture delivered in 1956 at The Frick Collection. An earlier and shorter version of the essay, submitted to the *Saggi e Memorie* of the Cini Foundation in August, 1959, has not yet been published because of unforeseen delays.

2 *Venetian Painting in America*, New York, 1910, pp. 95-105. Later F. J. Mather, Jr., advanced a similar view (*Venetian Painters*, New York, 1936, pp. 99-100). "The picture is a landscape," he says, "and as such offers no problems." To this he did add: "While the literal theme is the receiving of the stigmata, it is represented as a natural and benign event, like drawing a deep breath and realizing the lovely freshness of the morning."

3 Cf. *Italian Paintings and Drawings at 56 Princes Gate London SW 7* (ed. A. Seilern), London, 1959, II, p. 163. In the altarpiece, now in the Prado, painted after the *modello* in the Seilern Collection the saint looks up to the winged angel's head, which is much enlarged (F. J. Sánchez Cantón, *G. B. Tiepolo en España*, Madrid, 1953, pl. 25).

4 F. Kimball and L. Venturi, *Great Paintings in America*, New York, 1948, p. 58; also the *Catalogue of the Frick Collection*, Pittsburgh, I, 1949, pp. 238-241.

5 *Catalogue of the Treasures of the United Kingdom Collected at Manchester*, London, 1857, no. 194 (also: "The saint in the attitude of receiving the stigmata"); *Burlington Fine Arts Club, Early Venetian Pictures*, London, 1912, no. 26.

6 V. Moschini, *Giambellino*, Bergamo, 1943, p. 22; L. Dussler, *Giovanni Bellini*, Vienna, 1949, p. 89; Berenson, *loc. cit.; idem, Italian Pictures of the Renaissance*, Oxford, 1932, p. 71; A. Venturi, *Storia dell'arte italiana*, Milan, VII part 4, 1915, p. 310; R. Pallucchini, *Giovanni Bellini*, Milan, 1959, p. 140; and F. Hartt, "Carpaccio's *Meditation on the Passion*," *Art Bulletin*, XXII, 1940, p. 33.

7 R. van Marle, *Development of the Italian Schools*, The Hague, XVII, 1935, p. 268.

8 L. Venturi, *Pitture italiane in America*, Milan, 1931, pl. 294; P. Hendy, *Giovanni Bellini*, London, 1945, p. 27; G. Gronau, *Giovanni Bellini*, Stuttgart, 1930, pl. 84.

9 On the presence of Eyckian paintings in Padua and Venice see Meiss, "Jan van Eyck and the Italian Renaissance," in *Venezia e l'Europa, Atti del XVIII Congresso Internazionale di Storia dell'Arte*, Venice, 1956, pp. 62 ff., and R. Weiss, "Jan van Eyck and the Italians," *Italian Studies*, XI, 1956, pp. 1 ff. and XII, 1957, pp. 7 ff. On Bellini's study of panels by Roger van der Weyden see below, note 34.

10 For the technique of the Pesaro *Coronation* see C. Brandi, "The Cleaning of Pictures in Relation to Patina, Varnish, and Glazes," in *Burlington Magazine*, XCI, 1947, p. 183 ff., and *idem*, in *Bollettino del Istituto Centrale del Restauro*, 2, 1950, p. 57 ff.

11 In Mantegna's version of the *Agony* in London, which Bellini certainly knew, this tree stands at the right margin.

12 In this respect Mantegna's *Agony* in London is somewhat closer.

13 See the Appendix. Views about the date of this altarpiece were summarized by R. Pallucchini, *Catalogo della mostra di Giovanni Bellini*, Venice, 1949, p. 113.

14 G. Gronau, *Giovanni Bellini*, Berlin, 1930, p. 203.

15 Pallucchini, *Catalogo*, p. 140; R. Fry, *Giovanni Bellini*, London, 1899, p. 27.

16 The right hand of Bellini's St. Francis is anticipated by the right hand of his Redeemer (standing Man of Sorrows) in the National Gallery, London (Hendy, *op. cit.*, pl. 16).

[43]

17 The pantomime of all these figures, which includes an upward glance and the head turned back, is appreciably different from the demonstrative gesture of the Man of Sorrows with extended arms that appeared around 1360 (Meiss, *Painting in Florence and Siena After the Black Death*, Princeton, 1951, p. 124) and that may be found later in Mantegna's panel in Copenhagen.

    A gesture like Bellini's and Piero's, with a similar meaning of submission and acceptance, was given by Poussin to the Virgin in his late *Annunciation* in the National Gallery, London.

18 Pallucchini, *Catalogo*, fig. on p. 133.

19 See especially G. Robertson, "The Earlier Work of Giovanni Bellini," *Journal of the Warburg and Courtauld Institutes*, XXIII, 1960, pp. 45 ff.

20 See R. Longhi, "Piero dei Franceschi e lo sviluppo della pittura veneziana," *L'Arte*, XVII, 1914, pp. 246-249. In this important essay Longhi underestimated the significance of Flemish models for Bellini.

21 Meiss, "Jan van Eyck and the Italian Renaissance," pp. 63 ff.

22 Cf. L. Testi, *Storia della pittura veneziana*, Bergamo, I, 1909, fig. on p. 270.

23 See, for instance, *ibid.*, I, fig. on p. 405; II, figs. on pp. 353, 379.

24 Cf. J. Breck, *Art in America*, II, 1914, p. 280.

25 Already in the fourteenth century in Venice the throne is placed above the sun and moon, and enveloped by a *mandorla* — symbols that do not appear in Tuscany (cf. Meiss, *Painting in Florence*, p. 44).

    Longhi observed Bellini's rejection of the Venetian compositional tradition of the Coronation and suggested that he followed instead a lost Coronation by Piero or Melozzo that is reflected in Palmezzano's panel in the Brera (A. Venturi, *Storia dell'arte*, Milan, VII, part 2, 1913, fig. 56). Palmezzano's panel was made only at the end of the century, and provides scanty support for the hypothesis that such a Pieroan prototype ever existed.

26 Cf. the Vivarinesque representations in the Palazzo Comunale, Osimo (L. Testi, *op. cit.*, II, fig. on p. 392) and in the National Gallery, Washington (*Book of Illustrations*, Washington, 1941, p. 204).

    God the Father may appear in small Venetian panels too, as for instance the Vivarini school work in the Museo Civico, Turin (Testi, *op. cit.*, II, p. 377).

27 For the plateau composition see Meiss, "Jan van Eyck and the Italian Renaissance," pp. 64 ff., and *idem*, " 'Highlands' in the Lowlands; Jan van Eyck, the Master of Flémalle, and the Franco-Italian Tradition," *Gazette des Beaux-Arts*, LVII, 1961, pp. 273-314.

28 The scene of the Martyrdom of Peter also exhibits exceptional activity. The equestrian group of St. George in the Pesaro predella is likewise not adequately accounted for by the precedent of Jacopo Bellini.

29 See G. Pacchione, "Galleria e Museo della Ceramica di Pesaro," *Bollettino d'arte*, XXXI, 1937-38, pp. 117, 132.

30 This seems to be the painting that once was in the chapel of Marco Zorsi in S. Michele, Murano — a chapel built in 1475 and dedicated to the Resurrection in a notice of 1479 (cf. G. Ludwig and W. Bode, in *Jahrbuch der preussischen Kunstsammlungen*, XXIV, 1903, p. 131).

31 Berenson, *Venetian Painting in America*, pp. 95-105, dates the Pesaro altarpiece ca. 1475, the *Transfiguration* ca. 1480, the *Resurrection* around the same time or a little later, and then the Frick *St. Francis* just before the S. Giobbe altarpiece. L. Dussler, *loc. cit.*, dates the Frick picture about 1480, at the same time as the *Transfiguration*. The chronology of Hendy, *op. cit.*, p. 20 ff., is: Pesaro *Coronation*, *Resurrection* (1475), S. Giobbe altarpiece, *Earthly Paradise*, *Transfiguration*, and *St. Francis*. Longhi's order (*Burlington Magazine*, XCI, 1949, pp. 281-2) is: Pesaro ca. 1473, *Resurrection* (ca. 1479), *St. Francis*, Contini *St. Jerome*, *Transfiguration* (ca. 1485). Pallucchini (*Bellini*): Pesaro Altarpiece ca. 1470-1; *Resurrection*, 1475-9; Frick *St. Francis*; *Transfiguration*. G. Robertson (*op. cit.*, p. 55): Pesaro altarpiece, influenced by Antonello, shortly after 1475, *Resurrection*; the Frick panel and the *Transfiguration*, both around 1480.

32 See especially the immediate foreground of the *Transfiguration*.

[44]

33 J. Byam Shaw, "A Giovanni Bellini at Bristol," in *Burlington Magazine*, XCIV, 1952, p. 157. Shaw dates the work, a miniature on parchment, ca. 1473. The fact that the painting (which I have not seen) is a copy after Mantegna, even down to the drapery patterns of Christ, should not conceal the similarity of its style to the *St. Francis*.

In some of the paintings of this group — the *Resurrection* and the Contini *St. Jerome* — the share of the workshop seems to have been larger than in others. The *Resurrection*, furthermore, is not in good condition.

The common tendency to date the Frick panel late may have been due, at least in part, to the heavy yellow varnish that covered it until it was cleaned in 1042.

34 V. C. Habicht in *Belvedere*, X, 1931, pp. 54 ff., proposed that Bellini adopted two of Roger's figures. The Virgin in the *Nativity* of the Carità altarpiece was taken, he says, from a Rogerian model (not specified), and the Magdalen in the Pesaro *Crucifixion* from the Magdalen in Roger's *Lamentation*. The first observation is not convincing, the second very sound, but I have doubts about Bellini's authorship of this *Crucifixion*.

35 Bellini already had opportunities in Venice itself for the study of specimens of the work of Fra Filippo, Uccello, and Castagno (whose mosaic in the Mascoli Chapel must have had an effect on him during the 'seventies).

36 It is not, of course, exclusively Venetian, but in addition to the Bellinesque examples, others were made in the Veneto or in related styles. See for instance the panel in São Paulo attributed incorrectly to Mantegna (Berenson, *Vedere e Sapere*, Milan, n.d., pl. 55), several representations by Marco Zoppo, or the panel by Ercole de' Roberti in the Barlow Collection.

For observations on representations of St. Jerome in the Quattrocento cf. Hartt, *op. cit.*, p. 34. It seems to me unlikely, however, that, as Hartt says, the Venetian and Bellinesque compositions derive from Piero's panel now in the Accademia. They stem rather from a North Italian tradition represented by, for instance, Pisanello's panel in the National Gallery, London. Whereas Piero, in Central Italian fashion, raised the saint above the world, Pisanello immersed him in it. See also *St. Jerome*, close to Francesco dei Franceschi, Wildenstein and Co.

37 Cf. *Catalogue of the Paintings, Drawings, etc. in the Barber Institute of Fine Arts*, Cambridge, 1952, p. 8.

38 Hendy, *op. cit.*, pl. 107.

39 London, National Gallery (M. Davies, *The Earlier Italian Schools*, 1961, p. 71 and Pallucchini, *Giovanni Bellini, cit.*, p. 141, fig. 111) and Ashmolean Museum, Oxford.

40 *Ibid.*, pl. 109.

41 Cf. V. Golubew, *Die Skizzenbücher Jacopo Bellinis*, Brussels, 1912, II, pls. XIV and XXI.

42 Cf. Mantegna's early *Agony in the Garden*, London and *Parnassus* in the Louvre. In the latter the creature is in his hole, as in many earlier paintings. A rabbit appears alongside St. Francis in Giovanni del Biondo's *Stigmatization* in the altarpiece of the Rinuccini Chapel, S. Croce.

43 As Eugene Carroll kindly suggested to me. See the Golden Legend, s.v. Jerome (Sept. 30), and G. Kaftal, *Iconography of the Saints in Tuscan Painting*, Florence, 1952, p. 530 and fig. 608.

44 A. Venturi, *Storia dell'arte italiana*, Milan, VII, part 4, 1915, fig. 313.

If the representations of St. Jerome influenced the Frick *St. Francis*, it is also possible that the latter influenced at least one representation of the former: the picture by Veronese in the Art Institute, Chicago. In this painting there appear similarly disposed rocks and a tree, a lectern with a skull, a shepherd with his flock, and a city in the background.

45 In the Barlow Collection (G. Gronau, "Ercole dei Roberti's St. Jerome," *Burlington Magazine*, XCI, 1949, pp. 242-5) and, from the circle of Ercole, National Gallery, London.

46 See for example the Mantegnesque panel in the Museum at São Paulo, Brazil, cited in note 36.

47 The little crown of thorns, lacking in the *St. Jerome*, adorns the cross in Bellini's *Redeemer* in London.

48 "The Putto with the Death's Head," *Art Bulletin*, XIX, 1937, p. 430.

49 Though an entire skeleton is earlier associated with St. Francis, as in the Giottesque fresco in the lower church at Assisi (see F. Antal, *Florentine Painting and its Social Background*, London, 1948, pl. 82).

50 It appears on the saint's lectern in paintings by Bisi in the Pinacoteca Estense, Modena, and Murillo in the Convento de Capuchinos in Cádiz. It may be seen also in the *Stigmatization* by Rubens in the Wallraf-Richartz Museum, Cologne. See P. V. Facchinetti, *San Francesco d'Assisi*, Milan, 1921, pp. 403 ff.

51 Cf. the edition of Michiel by T. Frimmel, *Notizie d'opere di disegno nella prima metà del secolo XVI*, Vienna, 1888, p. 88. Berenson, construing "propinquo" as an adverb, believed the phrase meant "almost finished" ("propinquo finito") by Bellini, and he attributed part of the landscape to another painter (*Venetian Painting in America*, p. 104), but these views are certainly incorrect. L. Venturi, *Italian Paintings in America*, New York, 1933, no. 390, construes "propinquo" as "in the foreground."
This passage provides an early instance of the appearance of the concept of landscape ("paese"). On the history of this see E. H. Gombrich, "Renaissance Artistic Theory and the Development of Landscape Painting," in *Gazette des Beaux-Arts*, XLI, 1953, p. 335 ff.

52 Sometimes St. Francis, like St. Jerome, kneels before a book and a crucifix, with a skull alongside, but his hands are clasped in prayer (see Cigoli, Corsini and Borghese Galleries, Rome, and L. Carracci, Museo Capitolino). Often the saint flings his arms wide in ecstasy (painting attributed to Annibale Carracci, Museo Capitolino).

53 Villa I Tatti, Florence. Cf. J. Pope-Hennessy, *Sassetta*, London, 1939, pl. XXII.

54 See J. R. H. Moorman, *Sources for the Life of St. Francis*, Manchester, 1940, pp. 17-18, and P. Sabatier, *Vie de St. François d'Assise*, Paris, 1894, p. 348. K. Clark, *Landscape into Art*, London, 1949, p. 24, is speaking figuratively when he describes the painting as a "true illustration" of St. Francis' Hymn to the Sun.

55 Paintings in S. Francesco, Pescia; Uffizi; S. Francesco, Pistoia; three in the Pinacoteca, Siena, etc. (cf. Meiss, *Painting in Florence and Siena*, figs. 113-115).

56 Domenico Ghirlandaio, S. Trinita, Florence (Fig. 43; though the wound is not visible, its place is indicated by three small rays); Florentine late fifteenth century, Pinacoteca, Modena (Fig. 46); Barbagelata, Palazzo Bianco, Genoa (see G. V. Castelnovi, "Giovanni Barbagelata," in *Bollettino d'arte*, XXXVI, 1951, fig. 17).

57 Meiss, *op. cit.*, p. 119, note 56. For a standing St. Francis in a *Stigmatization* by Macrino d'Alba see Facchinetti, *op. cit.*, fig. on p. 408. I do not know those Venetian examples of the standing saint mentioned, without specification, by Berenson, *Venetian Painting in America*, p. 98.

58 For the entire panel see E. Tietze-Conrat, *Mantegna*, New York, 1955, fig. 16.

59 See the fresco now in the Municipio at Narni, dated 1528, by Lo Spagna.

60 *Paradiso*, XI, 106.

61 For the drawing by Jacopo Bellini see Golubew, *op. cit.*, II, pl. 67.

62 *Catalogue of the Frick Collection, cit.*, I, 1949, p. 239. Here it is pointed out also that at La Verna a massive rock rises from a meadow.

63 Van Marle, *loc. cit.*

64 Hendy, *op. cit.*, pl. 118. The donkey reappears, clearly with a specific iconographic motivation, under the arm of Silenus in Bellini's *Feast of the Gods* in Washington.

65 See Rabanus Maurus, in Migne, *Patr. lat.*, vol. 111, col. 212.

66 *Ibid.*, col. 246. Bellini's heron (apparently Ardea cinerea) lacks its crest. Nearby, what seems to be a little bittern (Ixobrychus minutus) lacks the creamy wing area.

67 The heron shuns carrion as the righteous the corrupt world. See E. P. Evans, *Animal Symbolism in Ecclesiastical Architecture*, London, 1896, p. 148.

68 Hugh of St. Victor, in Migne, *op. cit.*, vol. 177, col. 47. The gray heron symbolizes penitence, the white purity.

69 The vine with fruit appears of course in Bellini's late *Drunkenness of Noah* at Besançon.

70 F. Klauner, "Zur Symbolik von Giorgiones Drei Philosophen," in *Jahrbuch der Kunsthistorischen Samm-lungen*, LI, 1955, pp. 147 ff.
    Mantegna introduced the plants in, for example, the *Agony* in London, the *St. Sebastian* in the Louvre, and the *Adoration of the Magi* in the Uffizi.
    The fig alone appears in the Pesaro *Nativity*. Observing that it is most often represented in the Venetian region (Padua and Mantegna included), Klauner suggested that it, together with the cave in the Nativity, was an iconographic importation from the east after the fall of Constantinople, a rather dubious view.

71 For instance, in the *Psalter of Isabelle of France* (ed. S. C. Cockerell, London, 1905, pl. XVI) and Taddeo Gaddi's panel in the Accademia, Florence (see F. J. Mather, Jr., in *Art Studies*, VIII, 1931, fig. 5).

72 F. Hartt, *loc. cit.*, suggested that the movement of the tree in the Frick panel conveys a supernatural inter-vention.

73 Berchorius, *Reductorium Morale*, Cologne, 1730, I, pp. 495-496 (Bk. XII, chap. 84). The anthropomorphic laurel in Mantegna's late painting in the Louvre symbolizes "virtus deserta." The laurel was commonly con-nected with poetry, as in Boccaccio's *Life of Dante* (trans. by J. R. Smith, New York, 1901, p. 56).
    A similar laurel tree appears at the left margin of Bellini's *Crucifixion* in the Niccolini Collection (Fig. 60).

74 "Ista laurus significat crucem quam pro certo phebo id est Christo soli iustitiae fuerat dedicata ab eo corpo-raliter amplexata. . . ." (*Reductorium Morale*, bk. XV, quoted by W. Stechow, *Apollo and Daphne*, Leipzig, 1932, p. 3).

75 See the manuscript with North Italian miniatures of ca. 1400 in Gotha, Cod. membr. I, 98 (Stechow, *op. cit.*, p. 16 and figs. 10-11).

76 *Early Netherlandish Painting*, Cambridge (Mass.), 1953, I, p. 142.

77 See Meiss, "Light as Form and Symbol in Some Fifteenth-Century Paintings," *Art Bulletin*, XXVII, 1945, pp. 175-176, and F. Hartt, "Mantegna's *Madonna of the Rocks*," in *Gazette des Beaux-Arts*, XL, 1952, p. 329 ff.

78 Hendy, *op. cit.*, pl. 99.

79 *Ibid.*, pl. 113.

80 The recent cleaning of this painting has disclosed that this tree is heavily repainted.

81 *Ibid.*, pl. 94.

82 In the opinion of H. Olsen (*Federigo Barocci*, Uppsala, 1955, p. 151) this painting was executed by Barocci's studio.

83 Written about the middle of the fourteenth century.

84 The ministrations of this bird are described in the second *Considerazione*. Bartolommeo della Gatta, though a gifted painter, was not much of an ornithologist: he put an *owl* in the tree (Fig. 39).

85 *Actus B. Francisci et Sociorum Eius*, ed. P. Sabatier, Paris, 1902, p. 39. The image of La Verna lighted at the moment of the Stigmatization seems to have appeared first in an account of the event written in 1282 (cf. *Acta Sanctorum*, Oct. 11, col. 860): "Ad ipsius quoque crucifixi presentiam mons totus luce aurea refulgebat."

86 *I Fioretti di San Francesco*, ed. by F. Casolini, Milan, 1926, p. 232. The English translation given above is from the Everyman's Library edition, New York, 1951, p. 148.

87 The relationship of these figures to the shepherds at the Nativity needs no comment.

88 See K. Clark, *Piero della Francesca*, New York, 1951, fig. 55.

89 Dated 1528. The falcon is present also. The attribution to Lo Spagna is due to B. Berenson, *Central Italian Painters*, London, 1909, p. 254.

90 National Gallery, London. Cf. Hendy, *op. cit.*, pl. 94.

91 *Ibid.*, pl. 108.

92 *Ibid.*, pl. 99.

93 For sleeping figures in Venetian art cf. Meiss, *"Ovum Struthionis,"* in *Studies in Art and Literature for Belle Da Costa Greene*, ed. D. Miner, Princeton, 1954, p. 98.

94 Hendy, *op. cit.*, pls. 45-46.

95 See below, n. 117. In later art the seraph was sometimes just barely visible in the radiance in the sky, as in Guercino's painting in the Pinacoteca, Cesena. It appears indistinctly between the branches and leaves of a tree in a drawing by Barocci in the Uffizi. For a tiny angel's head instead of the seraph see above and note 116.

96 X-rays show very few changes. The largest one involves the position of the furthermost tree that grows from the rock.
    The panel was undoubtedly cut at the top because there the paint extends to the very edge of the panel whereas on the other three sides it stops about ½ inch short of the edge.

97 Noticed many years ago, it seems, by Adolfo Venturi, *Storia dell'arte italiana*, Milan, VII part 4, 1915, p. 310. It became much more apparent when the picture was cleaned in 1942.

98 *Last Judgment*, Hospital, Beaune; Braque triptych, Louvre; *Baptism*, Städel Institut, Frankfurt.

99 This opaque impasto is very different from the paint and glazes used in the rest of the surface, but close inspection has stilled my thought that this difference might signify lack of authenticity.

100 The church is large and rays are omitted. Cf. V. Golubew, *op. cit.*, I, pl. XLVII. In a drawing in the Louvre "sketchbook," the seraph is nearer and rays are represented (*ibid.*, II, pl. 67).

101 The church, a strange construction, is Romanesque except for what we may call the clerestory of the choir. Whether the position of the seraph above the Romanesque section and near the Gothic has a symbolic significance I would hesitate to say.

102 E. Tietze-Conrat, *Mantegna*, New York, 1955, pl. 25.

103 See Didron, *Christian Iconography*, London, 1886, II, p. 88, and H. Mendelsohn, *Die Engel in der bildenden Kunst*, Berlin, 1907, pp. 2,22. Miss Mendelsohn discusses the radiant angel but not the spectral angel of Bellini and his followers.

104 H. Olsen, *Italian Paintings and Sculpture in Denmark*, Copenhagen, 1961, p. 91, pl. VII.

105 See the *Death of the Virgin* in the Gesù, Cortona, and the *Last Judgment* in the Galleria Nazionale Barberini, Rome (formerly Corsini Collection).

106 Van Marle, *Development*, IV, fig. 210.

107 F. Wittgens, *Vincenzo Foppa*, Milan, n.d., pl. 79.

108 *A Catalogue of the Paintings at Doughty House, Richmond* (ed. H. Cook), London, 1915, III, no. 542 (pl.).

109 See O. Pächt, "A Giottesque Episode in English Medieval Art," *Journal of the Warburg Institute*, VI, 1943, p. 67.

110 In a related paper, "Light as Form and Symbol in Some Fifteenth-Century Paintings," in *Art Bulletin*, XXVII, 1945, pp. 175-181, I attempted to show that the ancient Christian association of light passing through a glass with the miraculous birth of Christ made its appearance in the visual arts only at a specific historical moment (ca. 1400), characterized by the appearance or development of other luminary subjects, and by the greatly quickened interest of painters in light in general. There, and in other writings as well as in the present paper, I have regarded iconography as responsive to form and as symbolic of deeper intrinsic meanings.

[48]

111 *Ibid.*, pp. 175-176.

112 Van Marle, *Development*, XI, 1929, fig. 154.

113 Matthew XVII, 1.

114 This new form takes its place alongside other Venetian sleeping figures — the Christ Child and Venus — that I have discussed elsewhere (see n. 93).

115 In a painting executed not more than a decade earlier, Paolo Uccello's *St. George* now in the National Gallery, London, the victory of the saint over the dragon occurs beneath a celestial disturbance.

116 See E. Mâle, *L'art religieux après le Concile de Trente*, Paris, 1932, p. 177.

117 The seraph does not appear in the Stigmatization in the fifteenth-century relief on the façade of S. Francesco, Piacenza, but the scene may have been cut down. P. V. Facchinetti, *Le Stimmate di San Francesco d'Assisi*, Milan, 1924, p. 112, says that the seraph is lacking in several representations of the Stigmatization, mostly of the sixteenth or seventeenth centuries. In all those I have been able to control, however, notably Bellini's Pesaro predella (Fig. 40), Pintoricchio's fresco in the Araceli, Rome, and Guercino's painting in the Pinacoteca Comunale, Cesena, the contrary is true.

118 See W. Friedlaender, *Caravaggio Studies*, Princeton, 1955, p. 26.

119 All this correspondence is given by J. Cartwright, *Isabella d'Este*, New York, 1923, I, pp. 341-358. For the letter of Bembo written January 1, 1506, see G. Gaye, *Carteggio inedito d'artisti dei secoli XIV, XV, XVI*, Florence, II, 1840, p. 71. For the correspondence see also C. Yriarte, "Isabella d'Este et les artistes de son temps," *Gazette des Beaux-Arts*, XV, 1896, p. 223.

120 Meiss, *Painting in Florence*, pp. 117-120.

121 The passage is quoted in *L'Alcoran des Cordeliers*, Amsterdam, 1784, I, p. 316.

122 Meiss, *op. cit.*, p. 120.

123 Cf. J. R. H. Moorman, *op. cit.*, p. 58. On the concealment of the wounds see chapter 98 of the *Second Life* of Tommaso da Celano.

124 *I Fioretti*, ed. F. Casolini, Milan, 1926, p. 232.

NOTES TO THE APPENDIX

125 *Rassegna d'arte*, II, 1915, p. 167.

126 *Beschreibendes Verzeichnis der Gemälde im Kaiser Friedrich-Museum*, Berlin, 1906, p. 443, no. 1170. It is here stated that two little panels of Sts. Martin and Lucy that were said to have come from Pesaro were perhaps parts of the predella. These panels were in the collection of Count U. Beni, Gubbio.

127 Its inventory number is 37.544. Mr. Edward S. King, director of the Walters Gallery, kindly informs me that it was bought by Henry Walters in Rome in 1902, as part of the Massarenti collection. (See E. Van Esbroeck, *Catalogue du musée de peinture, sculpture et archéologie au Palais Accoramboni*, Rome, 1897, no. 339 as Gentile da Fabriano. Also Marcello Massarenti, *Catalogue of Pictures, Marbles, Bronzes, etc., in the Palazzo Accoramboni*, Rome, 1894, no. 332 as Gentile da Fabriano.)

128 Vasari, ed. Milanesi, III, p. 406 (then in the "chiesa nuova di San Giovanni Evangelista"). See also *Catalogo delle pitture che si conservano nelle chiese di Pesaro*, Pesaro, 1783, p. 60 (a reference I owe to the kindness of Ulrich Middledorf). C. Malvasia, *Felsina Pittrice*, Bologna, 1841, I, p. 39, still places the altarpiece in the Chiesa Nuova, though it was in the Solly Collection as early as 1821, according to the Berlin catalogue (see note 126).

129 Conceivably the Man of Sorrows with two angels now in the Museum at Pesaro was the central pinnacle of the altarpiece (*Catalogo della esposizione della pittura ferrarese del Rinascimento*, Ferrara, 1933, no. 69). It is relatively very large (102 x 74 cm.) but it is similar in style and was once in the same church (see the *Catalogo* of 1783 cited in the preceding note). The point of sight is below the panel, implying a high position. Since these lines were written F. Zeri, *Paragone*, 107, 1958, p. 40 has come to the same conclusion.

130 See Pallucchini, *Giovanni Bellini*, p. 137, for the local tradition that the altarpiece was originally in this church.

131 The seraph has the usual position in the drawings in the Louvre (V. Golubew, *Die Skizzenbücher Jacopo Bellinis*, Brussels, 1912, II, pl. 67) and in London (*ibid.*, I, pl. 47). The figure in the latter is distant, small, and partly effaced, but Philip Pouncey, who very kindly examined it for me in 1955, reported that it is turned towards the Saint, and I have since been able to confirm this myself.

132 See above, p. 8.

133 Pallucchini, *op. cit.*, p. 57.

134 Testi, *op. cit.*, II, fig. on p. 357.

PLATES

Figure 1   Giovanni Bellini, *St. Francis.*
Frick Collection, New York

Figure 2   Giovanni Bellini, *St. Francis.* Detail. Saint and landscape at lower left.
Frick Collection, New York

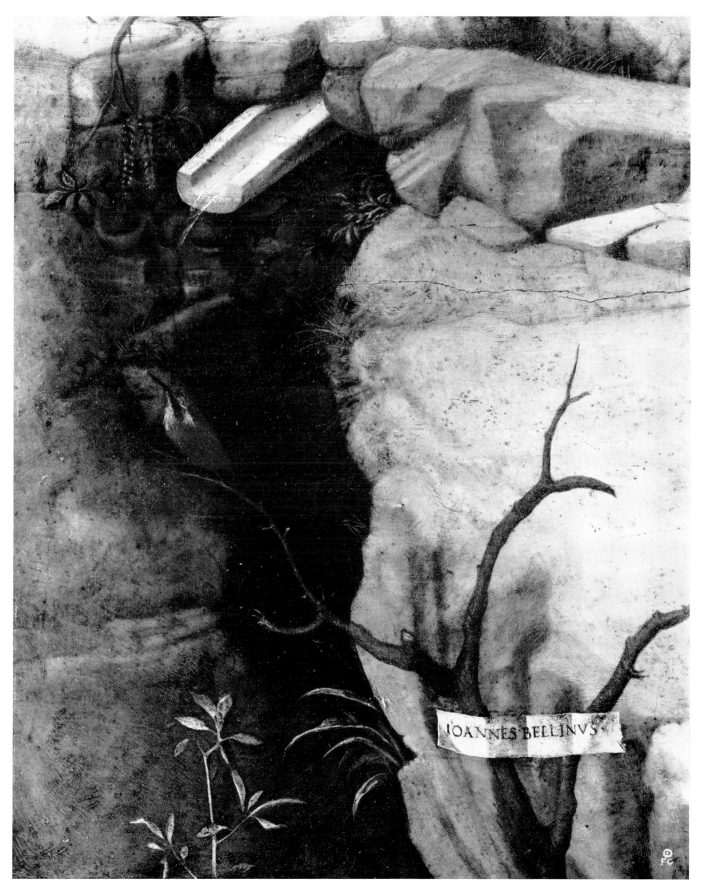

Figure 3   Giovanni Bellini, *St. Francis*. Detail. Spring, bittern, and signature.
Frick Collection, New York

Figure 4   Giovanni Bellini, *St. Francis*. Detail. Rocky landscape at lower left.
Frick Collection, New York

Figure 5   Giovanni Bellini, *St. Francis*. Detail. Sprouts beside laurel tree.
Frick Collection, New York

Figure 6   Giovanni Bellini, *St. Francis*. Detail. Shepherd with his flock, gray heron, and donkey.
Frick Collection, New York

Figure 7   Giovanni Bellini, *St. Francis*. Detail. Plum tree and plants at left of Saint.
Frick Collection, New York

Figure 8   Giovanni Bellini, *St. Francis*. Detail. Castle above stream.
Frick Collection, New York

Figure 9   Giovanni Bellini, *St. Francis.* Detail. Laurel tree and radiance in sky.
Frick Collection, New York

Figure 10 Giovanni Bellini, *St. Francis*. Detail. Briar, broken fig tree, and rabbit.
Frick Collection, New York

Figure 11   Giovanni Bellini, *St. Francis*. Detail. The Saint and his garden.
Frick Collection, New York

Figure 12   Giovanni Bellini, *St. Francis*. Detail. Rocks, river, and distant hills.
Frick Collection, New York

Figure 13   Giovanni Bellini, *St. Francis*. Detail. St. Francis.
Frick Collection, New York

Figure 14   Giovanni Bellini, *St. Francis*. Detail. Mullein, juniper, and orris root at right of Saint.
Frick Collection, New York

Figure 15   Giovanni Bellini, *St. Francis*. Detail. Lectern and cell.
Frick Collection, New York

Figure 16   Giovanni Bellini, *St. Francis*. Detail. Flowers, vines, and
trees above central rocks.

Frick Collection, New York

Figure 17   Giovanni Bellini, *St. Francis*. Detail. Spleenwort and other plants above cell.

Frick Collection, New York

Figure 18 Giovanni Bellini, *St. Francis*. Detail. Maidenhair fern and English ivy on large rock. Frick Collection, New York

Figure 19   Giovanni Bellini, *St. Francis*. Detail. Landscape at top left.
Frick Collection, New York

Figure 20   Giovanni Bellini, *St. Francis*. Detail. Grapevine above cell.
Frick Collection, New York

Figure 21   Giovanni Bellini, *St. Francis*. Detail. Rays in upper left corner.
Frick Collection, New York

Figure 22   Giovanni Bellini, *St. Francis*. Detail. Castle at top center.
Frick Collection, New York

Figure 23   Titian, *Pesaro Altarpiece*. Venice, Frari

Figure 24 Mantegna, *Agony in the Garden*. Tours, Musée des Beaux-Arts

Figure 25 Fra Filippo Lippi, *Madonna*.
Florence, Uffizi

Figure 26 Giovanni Bellini, *Descent into
Limbo*. Bristol, City Art Gallery

Figure 27   Giambono, *Stigmatization of St. Francis* (detail).
Venice, Count Vittorio Cini

Figure 28   Giovanni Battista Tiepolo,
Stigmatization of St. Francis (detail).
London, Count A. Seilern

Figure 29   Piero della Francesca,
Members of a Confraternity (detail of *Madonna*).
Borgo Sansepolcro, Museo

Figure 30   Antonello da Messina, *Crucifixion* (detail).
London, National Gallery

Figure 31   Giovanni Bellini, *Coronation of the Virgin*. Pesaro, Museo Civico

Figure 32   Giovanni Bellini, *Coronation of the Virgin* (detail). Pesaro, Museo Civico

Figure 33　Giovanni Bellini (assisted), *Resurrection*. Berlin-Dahlem, Museum Dahlem

Figure 34 Giovanni Bellini (assisted), *St. Jerome*. Florence, Contini Collection

Figure 35   Carlo Crivelli, *St. Jerome*.
London, National Gallery

Figure 36   Giovanni Bellini, *St. Jerome* (predella of
Fig. 31). Pesaro, Museo Civico

Figure 37   Giovanni Bellini, *St. Jerome*.
Birmingham, Barber Institute

Figure 38   Garofalo, *The Baptist*.
Cambridge, Fitzwilliam Museum

Figure 39   Bartolommeo della Gatta, *Stigmatization of St. Francis.*
Castiglion Fiorentino, Pinacoteca

Figure 40   Giovanni Bellini, *Stigmatization of St. Francis* (predella of Fig. 31).
Pesaro, Museo Civico

Figure 41   Site of the Stigmatization, La Verna

Figure 42   Marco Zoppo, *Stigmatization of St. Francis.* Baltimore, Walters Gallery

Figure 43   Domenico Ghirlandaio, *Stigmatization of St. Francis.* Florence, S. Trinita

Figure 44   Giovanni Bellini, *Agony in the Garden*. London, National Gallery

Figure 45   Follower of Guido da Siena,
Stigmatization of St. Francis. Siena, Pinacoteca

Figure 46   Florentine, late fifteenth
century, *Stigmatization of St. Francis*.
Modena, Galleria Estense

Figure 47   Barocci (assisted), *Stigmatization of St. Francis*. Florence, Uffizi

Figure 48   Ercole de' Roberti, *Agony in the Garden*.
Dresden, Gemäldegalerie

Figure 49   Giovanni Bellini,
Agony in the Garden (detail of Fig. 44).
London, National Gallery

Figure 50   Dirk Bouts, *God the Father*
(detail of *Gathering of Manna*).
Louvain, St. Peter's

Figure 51   Mantegna (?), *Stigmatization of St. Francis*
(detail of a panel). Boston, Gardner Museum

Figure 52 Ambrogio Lorenzetti, *Angels*
(detail of the *Madonna*). Siena, Pinacoteca

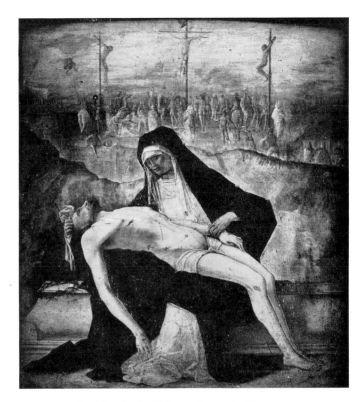

Figure 53 Ercole de' Roberti, *Vesperbild*.
Liverpool, Walker Art Gallery

Figure 54 The Bedford Master, *Agony in the
Garden*. British Museum, Add. 18850, fol. 208

Figure 55 Tura, *Vesperbild*.
Venice, Museo Correr

Figure 56   Bronzino, *Stigmatization of St. Francis.*
Florence, Cappella dell' Eleanora, Palazzo Vecchio

Figure 57   Florentine Mosaic, late thirteenth century,
Pharaoh's Dream. Florence, Baptistery

Figure 58   Moretto, *Conversion of St.
Paul.* Milan, S. Maria sopra S. Celso

Figure 59   Orazio Gentileschi (?), *Stigmatization of St.
Francis* (?). Rome, Colonna Gallery

Figure 60   Workshop of Giovanni Bellini, *Crucifixion*.
Florence, Collection Count Niccolini

Figure 61   Giovanni Bellini, *Transfiguration*. Venice, Museo Correr

Figure 62   Giovanni Bellini, *Transfiguration*. Naples, Museo di Capodimonte

Figure 63   Marco Zoppo, Altarpiece. Formerly Berlin, Kaiser Friedrich Museum (burnt in 1945)